ALL ABOUT DECORATING

BY DENNIE HOUGHTON CARTER
AND THE EDITORS OF
1,001 DECORATING IDEAS

CONSO PUBLISHING COMPANY·NEW YORK

FOREWORD

ALL ABOUT DECORATING is the result of the combined efforts of many individuals — from the home furnishing manufacturers to the editors of 1,001 DECORATING IDEAS magazine and the interior designers who combined those ingredients wisely and well. We'd like to list all the interior designers whose works are shown on our pages, and give a special thank you to Contributing Editor Rose Bennett Gilbert for her expert assistance with the compilation and writing.

INTERIOR DESIGNERS

ETHYL G. ALPER, A.I.D.

GEOFFREY BEENE

DAVID EUGENE BELL, A.I.D.

EVERETT BROWN, F.A.I.D.

MICHAEL CANNAROZZI

PEDRO D. CANO, A.I.D., ASSOC.

DENNIE H. CARTER, N.H.F.L.

MARY CHURCH, N.H.F.L.

EUGENIA DEAN, N.S.I.D.

JAMES DE MARTIN

JAY DORF, A.I.D.

JESSIE DRUSS, A.I.D.

ARDINE GOSS, A.I.D.

T. MILES GRAY ASSOCIATES, N.S.I.D., A.I.D.

ANTHONY HAIL

ALBERT E. HERBERT, JR., A.I.D.

ROBERT W. HOUSEMAN, A.I.D., ASSOC.

PAUL H. KRAUSS, III, A.I.D.

EMILY MALINO, A.I.D., N.H.F.L.

JEROME I. MANASHAW, A.I.D.

ELLEN LEHMAN MCCLUSKEY, F.A.I.D.

GUY MONYPENNY

JAMES CHILDS MORSE, A.I.D.

EDMUND MOTYKA, A.I.D.

GEORGE PECK

SHIRLEY REGENDAHL, N.H.F.L.

JULEEN SEESE

ROBERT SHROYER

WILLIAM B. STOREY, A.I.D.

EDMUND TAAKE

ARCHIBALD TAYLOR, F.A.I.D.

ANDY THOMPSON, N.S.I.D.

RAYMOND WARK, A.I.D.

DOUGLAS W. WILLIAMSON

BEBE WINKLER

THOMAS A. WOODS, A.I.D.

DEPARTMENT STORES

RICH'S, ATLANTA

BLOOMINGDALES, NEW YORK

ALTMAN'S, NEW YORK

G. FOX, HARTFORD

L. S. AYRES, INDIANAPOLIS

CONTENTS

I

AT THE BEGINNING

Back up for a whole new look at this topic of interior design. Decorating is a fine art and a fun art. Fine, because it embraces almost all the other arts man has ever made to beautify his environment, from painting to fine furniture, textiles, tapestries and a thousand et ceteras. A well-done room, thoroughly thought through and finished, can be a work of art as pleasing as any poem or painting—it's "chamber" music, indeed. In the process, you become a kind of artist—a homemaker, not housekeeper, and environment planner instead of mere purchasing agent. Although such job descriptions may smack of our twentieth-century trend toward trumped-up titles, merely by filling living space with furnishings—tables to eat from, chairs to sit upon, curtains to keep out glare and stares—you are indeed creating an environment in which your family will live happily.

Environment has shown itself to be a mighty molder, affecting directly our outlook and attitudes. Simply put, pleasant rooms make pleasant people. At least, they make pleasant people more so. Don't pale, Environment Planner. Even with psychology mixed into decorating, there's no need to be overawed by the job ahead. No need to speak reverently of "Louis This" or "Provincial That." Or to apologize if your funds are few. Somehow, sadly, this whole subject of interior design has become submerged in its own mystique, so people approach it with fear and timidity, insecure in their own tastes, yet afraid to engage a professional designer. So the whole exciting, colorful art of decorating settles into a lump of awesome responsibility.

Instead, decorating is a fun art, fun in the doing and fun to live with and look at afterward. By its very nature—the designing of our home interiors so they are pleasant places to be—decorating is a hospitable art, one of the most social graces. And, in the same social context, it follows that we judge and are judged by our homes. They're visible extensions of the way we live and think...of the colors we like, of the formal or informal life we lead. Despite the mystique that sometimes surrounds it, successful

Decorating is never done forever, for tastes do change as time marches on. These two living rooms were photographed in the editor's own home just a decade apart. But during that time the homey all-Early American mood, manifest above in warm woods and a folksy print, has taken a sophisticated turn toward Modern, apparent in setting and accessories opposite.

decorating really has nothing to do with snobbery, little to do with money and heirlooms. Energy and taste are the major ingredients in good decorating. You'll need the former to develop the latter...and to keep up with its changes through the years. For your tastes will, indeed, change as you live, look and

learn more about this ever-changing field. The two pictures on these pages are truly worth thousands of words when it comes to proving the point. Such change is as exciting as it is inevitable, another reason this fine art of decorating is such a fun, fun art. It is also a highly personal art. Its whole objective is to be subjective. Even if you turn the job

Designed by Edward Durell Stone, with sweeping expanses of glass and a flowing floor plan, the house above demands a streamlined decorating style, although some of the earlier furnishings still fit (in the dining area, for example). Welcome— and expect—such changes in tastes and life styles. They keep a home as up-to-date and vital as the family who lives there.

completely over to a professional designer, you'll find him going right back to this basic starting point: What do *you* like? How do *you* like to live? With large dinner parties that demand dining space for 12? Or with the emphasis on more informal living. For example, we've moved our dining area into the large living room of our current house because it suits our more casual way of entertaining. Perhaps you'd like a game corner in your living room. A bar? Or is TV important to your happiness? Should it be a main living room feature? Or would you prefer it tucked away in a den?

Analyze your tastes and distastes, the living habits that will affect your habitat. Remember that a home

Choosing a furnishing style is more a matter of choosing a mood than a definite historical period. Four of the most popular approaches include the informal look, typified by Early American, left, with its colorful, homespun coziness. The provincial feeling, right, is flavored with French for a kind of easy sophistication that includes painted wood, pewter and plaids.

is to live in, not just look at. You are out to create much more than mere one-dimensional loveliness.

You are developing that environment in which you and your family will function happily. Once you have self-understanding in hand, you know where you're going. Getting there is, indeed, *more* than half the fun. There's a bright new world of fashion, fact and fancy ahead, and both your esthetics and your intellect are in for a pleasant polishing once you step into it. Follow furniture styles back through time and emerge with an impressive, practical understanding of antiques...and of man's advancing

civilization. Look ahead to the almost science-fiction world of fabrics and fibers *already* available today. Overall, enjoy the glamor, the élan of this fine, fun art of decorating. You'll feel it in the sheer excitement of color, the sensuousness of textures, the interplay of shapes and sizes, curves and angles. Step by step, room by room, we'll show you how to appreciate decorating as an art. And how to practice it as a domestic science, to adapt it to your own life style so that your home tells at a glance who you are, how you live, what you like.

Suppose you don't know what you really like? Then take a good look all around you—when you

Take the English approach and you're in for elegance tempered by quiet, good taste, left. Look for dark, rich woods, oriental rugs, a lot of polished brass. The Modern-minded want slick and shine and see-through, furnishings that reflect the fast pace of today's technology and life style. Designs are sharp, colors clear, materials highly, handsomely functional.

visit friends, when you go furniture-store browsing, when you leaf through magazines and newspapers. Build up a working file of ideas as you go. Clip pictures of furniture styles. Include your own notes on interesting arrangements or color schemes you've seen on a charity-house tour or in the model rooms of a department store. Add swatches of fabric (with a note on price and source), and a sample of paint or a bit of fringe that caught your eye. Use your file like a "brain-storming" session—no fair censoring what goes in *when* it goes in. The rambling assortment, representing many moods and impulses, will reveal lots about your likes and dislikes when you finally bring them out for study. The first step after you analyze your tastes and family-life patterns is to accept them as they really are, then be practical in building your decor around them. If you love chintz, have chintz! Or put in Plexiglas chairs, if they're more you and never mind your mother-in-law's homage to antiques.

On the other hand, if yours is a leather-and-steel kind of family, don't try to superimpose even the most elegant brocade on them. You'd just be putting up a false front. And putting satin slipcovers on the TV sofa is deliberately declaring war on young children.

Don't. Neither you nor they will ever enjoy your best decorating efforts.

Step two: Accept realities. You aren't decorating a castle in Spain. You're dealing with a 12-by 18-foot living room, a pair of mismatched windows, a spiteful old radiator, cookie-eating kids, untrained puppies, etc. You will doubtless be dealing with old possessions, too: the too-good-to-get-rid-of sofa, the made-to-fit draperies, the saggy-bottomed reading chair you couldn't live without. These liabilities are really assets in disguise, for they provide a framework for your overhauling job.

If you are working with a designer, don't fear that he'll demand a clean-sweep either—most of the professionals are happy to work your cherished old things right into the new plan. Otherwise, you might do everything over in one burst of enthusiasm, leaving little room and less money to make changes as your tastes do. Which brings us right up against the third and most sobering reality—the budget. Know before you begin what you have to spend, right now and in the long run. Taste need not be expensive. Some of the best things in your rooms will be free, or nearly so—the good furniture arrangement, a great color scheme, etc. But the smartest budget rule is still: "Buy the best you can afford." Certain items should be looked on as investments and paid for accordingly. Buy a quality sofa. Buy the finest beds you can. Count on a good carpet's longevity to offset its cost. Before you spend a cent, spend lots of time learning about what you're buying. Read about the new miracle fabrics; study the insides of well-built furniture; do what the business world calls a "cost analysis" (i.e., price-vs.-life).

And now that you've accepted those inevitable prerequisites to decorating, turn rebel! *Refuse* to accept all the ideas you've simply been taking for granted all these years. Re-examine your prejudices against, say, plastics. Things have changed—and are changing—dramatically, excitingly, on the home-furnishings front. In this, the almost twenty-first century, *we* can have stainless steel furniture and stretch fabrics, glass walls and fluorescent lighting. Colonial Williamsburg couldn't. Why must we fill our homes with furnishings from yester-century when all around us men are going to the moon and making miracle fabrics? If you probe down inside your prejudices and honestly decide that you prefer chintz and Chippendale, then you should stick with it. But too often we go on repeating what we know without investigating what we don't know. And once you start looking into the excitement of today's offerings, you'll be amazed at what you missed.

Design ideas have changed right along with our technology, and you must be prepared to change, too, to think new! think now! Such thinking leads naturally to a rebellion against finality in furnishing your home. Long gone is the unalterable, formal parlor. Don't plan to furnish, finish and then spray-net a room into place forever. Build a bit of flexibility into your plan (and into your budget), so you'll feel free to rework parts of the room's decor in the future to reflect your changing needs and ideas. Change is the one constant force in our lives, and one of the most delightful. Who would dare declare anything finished (except the dishes) if you

Why keep returning to yesteryear's furnishings when Today can be so exciting to look at, so easy to live with? This of-the-moment recreation room is based on danceable resilient flooring and features sculptured furniture, floor cushions and plastic tables.

knew you could never go back and make any changes? Such finality has no place in decorating today. Rooms and families thrive on change. Even "fads," formerly taboo in most decorating circles, have something good to be said about them—a *little bit* of a fad can add a lot of new life to a room. A generous sprinkling of bright pillows—a 1970 fad—can make a room look like NOW but can easily be packed away tomorrow. If your initial investments—sofa, carpets, etc.—are good, you can afford a bit of playfulness. Besides, it will keep you from being afraid of taking off on a decorating venture if you

know you're not unalterably, irretrievably committed. That's why it's good to keep a few "replaceables" in your plan, that hand-me-down table, an inexpensive footstool, a canvas sling chair.

Don't hesitate to use such unimportant—but attractive—items to fill in between your good things, while you're working your way up to all "good" things. Spray-painted wicker baskets make splendid end tables; a cluster of greens can fill a bare corner dramatically; magazines yield nice frame-ables for a naked wall, etc., etc., to the ends of your imagina-

tion. The pages that follow are full of such fresh ideas. If you wait till you can afford the best of everything, you'll spend a long time with nothing.

Doubtless, you'll fall forever in love with some of your interim objects and never move them into the attic or the extra room. But lest you forget your overall objectives, commit your decorating plans to paper. Writing things down often clarifies them.

A blueprint also gives the rest of the family a preview of what's coming, so they can approve or make amendments. Such written details, plus a scale drawing of your room, are essential equipment if you're planning to work with a professional designer, who will want to know as much as possible about your home and about you before he begins. In turn, you may

More decorating sense than dollars adds up attractively in this young couple's first home. Bright colors, paint and slipcovers conceal the Salvation Army genealogy of most of the furnishings.

have questions about the professional designer—what he knows, what he can do for your home, what he's likely to charge and where you can find him. To begin with, the professional designer is exactly that, a person who is trained and skilled in designing interiors. He can discuss your tastes and needs with you and turn them into attractive, practical room plans with furniture, fabrics, colors and accessories

all worked out. Then, if you like, he will follow through, ordering, and installing your new decor.

Or, you can draw up your own plans, bringing in the designer as a consultant who will help solve specific problems, say, what treatment for a tricky window. The designer knows both his decorating history and the current market—what's available where. He also knows where to go for antiques and for custom work, saving you inches of shoe leather and hours of shopping time. His expertise, bought in the beginning of your decorating venture, may well save you dollars, too—dollars you might waste on the wrong fabric, poor quality furniture, a fake antique.

All this knowledge is the result of both formal training and professional practice, at least for members of the American Institute of Interior Designers (AID) and the National Society of Interior Designers (NSID). Both professional organizations require their members to have college-level training and five years' experience, plus a sound business record. Those initials behind a designer's name are like Ph.D. behind a teacher's—you're sure you're dealing with someone who knows his business. Both AID and NSID will furnish names of member designers in your area if you query their New York City headquarters (see Glossary). Or you may find a designer through the decorating department of a store, through a friend or from the yellow pages in your phone book (ask to see work samples).

Methods and amounts of payment will vary, too. A designer gets his fee in several ways. He may charge you the same retail price you'd pay anywhere for the furniture, fabrics, etc. you buy to implement his design plan. Since he can buy at special prices, he collects the difference. In essence, his services are therefore free to you, except for custom designs, special projects, etc. Other designers charge a fixed fee for their services, set in advance and dependent on how well-known and how busy he is. Still others charge a percentage of the total cost of the furnishings you buy at his direction. Since this figure is often 10 per cent, decorators who operate this way are known as "Ten-Percenters"—and they are frowned upon by the professional organizations who say this method short-changes both parties.

If you find a designer through the decorating department of a store, you may pay no fee, as such, at all. You do agree to make your purchases through the store and you usually have to make a deposit which will later be applied against those purchases. This is not a hindering arrangement since the stores can place special orders for fabrics, carpets, etc., and have other items specially made.

Suppose you've worked out your own plan, chosen almost everything and just want assurance before you spring open your check book and start buying? Then buy just enough of a designer's time to talk out your anxieties. He's available for $25 an hour and up, but if $25 is all you want to spend, be prepared to take your plans to him. "House calls" will probably cost more. Discuss and agree in advance on how much the designer will be paid, and how much you want to spend overall.

Thus, at the beginning, whether you're off on your own or with a designer, you have homework to do—a few rules to learn, a new language to sample, a lot of fun ahead. By the time you reach the Glossary at the back of this book you'll learn all you need to know about "Louis This" and "Provincial That," about color and windows and every room in your house. At least 1,001 decorating ideas are waiting …so on to the least expensive, most exciting, and, too often, most frightening idea of all—color.

A professional designer can help you create the look you want, within the budget you have. Case in point: this pair of elegant French-inspired bedrooms. The one above cost a whopping $30,000 for its $85-a-yard silk brocade fabric, handmade trimmings and $790-worth of imported velvet on the walls. The rare antiques are priceless, but you can have the look of it all for a mere $3,000, the cost of the entire room at right. Wide-wale corduroy on the walls, stock trims and French reproductions are substituted, and the room loses nothing in translation—except $27,000.

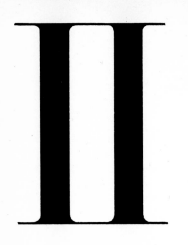

COLOR YOUR ROOMS EXCITING

Psychologists may tell us that some of our dreams are in black-and-white, but most interior designers would disagree. *Color* is the stuff that dream rooms are made of. Color, the magic medium that costs less and does more than any other ingredient in your decorating plans. Raise the roof, warm a room, shrink a sofa—you can do it all with a spin of the color wheel, once you understand what makes it go 'round.

There's no great mystery to the magic of color, even if you weren't born with the proverbial "eye" for it. All you do is develop the eye you have, to learn to look at the thousands of colors around you every day and see the ones you'd like to live with at home. It's as easy and exciting as assembling a new outfit, yet this is where the

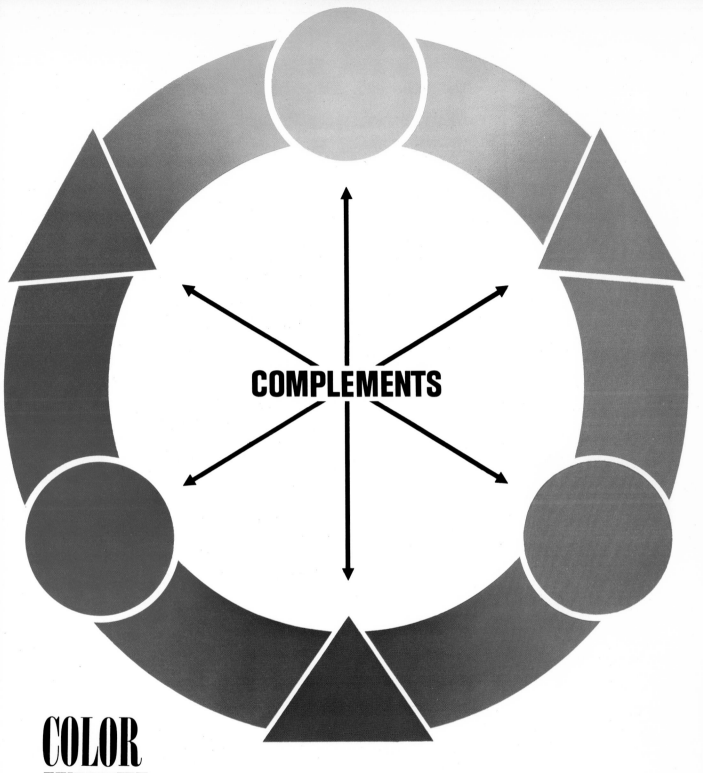

COMPLEMENTS

COLOR WHEEL

revolves around the three primary colors—yellow, red and blue—the three colors that can be mixed in varying proportions to produce any other color in the rainbow. In decorating, these primaries can be used together if you are deliberately seeking to create a scintillating scheme, perhaps as in a child's room. So you begin mixing colors around the wheel to produce compatible combinations. Equal amounts of two primaries create the secondary colors: orange, violet and green. Color technicians take the divi-

sions on to the third (tertiary) and fourth (quaternary) levels. But home decorators are more interested in turning the color wheel into the most attractive schemes for their rooms. There are three major types: related, complementary and monochromatic. Related colors fall between two primary colors on the wheel, e.g., green is related to blue and yellow. Complementary colors lie opposite each other on the wheel and are unalike but lively together. Monochromatic color schemes start with any one color and mix in black or white (the un-colors) for a variety of intensities.

amateur is most likely to panic. There are definite directions for using color, alone and in patterns. These black-and-white formulae have been developed by professionals and proved over and over again. Following these formulae, you can build any of the three basic color schemes that have been found to produce the most pleasing rooms: monochromatic, related and complementary.

We'll analyze them in a minute; meanwhile, don't think you'll be a dull copycat to follow these leads. Once you plug your individual color choices into whichever formula you prefer, it will become very personally yours. Success is almost certain, *if* you start off with workable color choices. To guarantee that, you need a working knowledge of colors, how they behave physically, optically and emotionally when they are used in varying proportions, under various conditions. This calls for research into the nature of color itself, and will bring forth a whole new vocabulary, one you'll hear in every conversation about color, especially if you work with a professional designer.

First, sweep aside all the fanciful adjectives, the "kumquats," "absinthes" and "aubergines." You'll find a very simple set of colors behind them all: red, yellow and blue. Every other color under the sun starts as one of these three, known as the *primary colors.* Traditionally, these are spaced equidistantly around a circle, the *color wheel,* and the space between filled with the colors produced by mixing them in equal amounts: red and yellow make orange; yellow and blue equal green; blue and red produce violet. Orange, green and violet are the *secondary colors.* Such colors, containing visible amounts of a primary color, are *related* to it, as all greens are related to both blue and yellow (but not to red); oranges to both yellow and red (but not blue); purples to red and blue (but not yellow). Such relationships are harmonious ones, and the families get on well when they are composed into a room setting. *Related color schemes,* therefore, are usually restful and refreshing. Keep on mixing around the wheel and you can come up with any color—to match your eyes, the flower in any fabric, the design on your antique china collection, etc. Going around the perimeter of the wheel this way, you are working with pure colors, or *hues,* as they are also called.

Colors go in other directions, too. Directly across from each hue on the wheel lies its *complement,* the color most unlike it. Red and green, yellow and violet, orange and blue are all complements. Mix them in equal amounts and you will get gray, for they neutralize each other. Use them side by side, however, and you get instant vigor, combinations that set the eye vibrating. Because of this, *complementary color schemes* are the liveliest of the three basic plans and must be well-balanced to be successful.

Another dimension of color is called *intensity* (or tone or chroma), that is, how red is the "red" you are considering—fire engine bright or pale as pink. Both are officially "red"; the difference is in the intensity. Color is also measured in terms of its *value,* i.e., its lightness or darkness. Yellow has a higher value than chartreuse, chartreuse than violet, etc. Colors close to white in value are called *tints;* those close to black are called *shades.* It's the variety of intensities and values that give interest to a *monochromatic* (one-hue) *color scheme.*

Finish is another physical dimension of color. A lustrous, shiny finish—on a lacquered Parsons table, for example, will appear much lighter than a color with a mat, or dull, surface. Satin pillows will look brighter than the velvet sofa cover they were dyed to match. Size and space affect color, too—the larger the area and the closer you are to it, the brighter the color appears. Remember this and get *large* samples of paint and fabric that you can put up and walk away from, the way an artist steps back from his easel. Take another cue from the Impressionist painters who made art history out of an optical illusion. The eye, they realized, automatically mixes colors used close together. A dab of blue beside green is seen as turquoise, both on canvas and in your living room. So instead of the blue-and-green tweed rug you thought you bought, you can end up with all-wrong turquoise underfoot. Nor can you always believe your eyes even when colors are used separately if they are seen together. A green chair, for example, looks much greener on a red rug. Red and green are *complements,* remember? Move that chair against a yellow wall and instantly it's softer. Green and yellow are *related* colors, remember? The eye will also meld colors in small-patterned fabrics and wallpapers, sometimes with decor-spoiling effects.

HARNESS THE POWER OF COLOR

It can push your walls around with the greatest of ease to fool the eye into seeing a "long, narrow" room, above, or a "square" one, below. The warm melon wall asserts its presence and seems to push forward into the room, while blue recedes quietly into the distance, aided by the green lines along the ceiling that catch and carry the eye along.

The quality and quantity of the light in your room can also throw your colors all out of key. Time was when shoppers automatically took their choice to the door of the store "to see it in the light" and determine its true color. Still a good idea if you're shopping for outdoor furnishings. Otherwise, evaluate colors in the room under the conditions in which they will live. The red that looks so sharp and zippy in the store might go too blue at home in your northern exposure. The green that fairly screams under the shop's fluorescent lights might warm up amazingly in the afternoon sun your guest room gets. Now's the time to lean on your understanding of the differences in the *values* of various colors, i.e., how much built-in light or dark they have. You must also appreciate the effects of artificial light on colors. Most incandescent bulbs cast a warm yellowish glow; fluorescent lights are generally cold blue-white. Both can play astonishing games with colors.

COOL *to the eye and the emotions, white trimmed with crisp green puts a summer-fresh face on the bedroom, left. Light colors, smooth textures and frothy fabrics at the window and on the bed contribute to the overall "air-conditioned" effect. The only furniture changes are in the headboard and picture over the bedside table. Otherwise, color is the major coolant.*

WARM *and cozy in its wintertime wear, the same bedroom, below, shows how color can create a climate. Red, which looks warm all by itself, gets a little extra insulation from the snug-underfoot lionskin rug and the quilted spread and headboard. There, the print fabric is fired with hot pink to generate a little life-giving busyness, always more welcome in winter than summer.*

The nature and color of a lamp shade will also influence the tone of the light it gives. So will the nature and color of the room's ceiling and walls, since the light usually bounces off them and back over the colors in the room. By studying large color samples "on location" you should automatically account for these many variables that will affect the way they will look after your room is done.

Now consider the effect the colors in a room can have on you. Colors evoke emotions. Our language is rich with clichés to attest to that—we feel "blue," or "in the pink"; "see red," go "purple with rage," "green with envy," etc. Everyone has a different reaction to different colors, but there are some generalities you should understand. First, each color has a climate—either it's *warm* or *cool*. Our psychological associations here have an obvious physical base, and that's Nature itself.

The warm colors are the colors of the sun, of fire, of anger or excitement: oranges, yellows, reds. Cool colors are found in the shade, in the evening, in quiet repose: blues, greens, violets. Translated into a room setting, these colors keep their emotional properties. If you want a cheerful, convivial room with a very today look, bring on the warm colors in broad sweeps. Conversely, cool, light colors are conducive to relaxation and quiet talk. The subtler, dignified tones usually work better in traditional rooms. That may be because our bright modern dyes just weren't available to the likes of Louis XV, but since we're used to seeing the soft, grayed tones in sumptuous settings, we equate them with elegance and sophisti-

cation. That goes for pastels, too (outside the nursery). By comparison, the bright, bold, clear colors seem more contemporary, more informal. Indeed, they are more "aggressive," more likely to make their presence felt in a room. Children love them; men usually don't, preferring the darker tones. Because women, in general, tend toward light tints and soft hues, you should honor your family's feelings when you're planning a den or playroom.

However, you can harness the "aggressiveness" of strong colors for surprising tasks—lower a ceiling, "cozy up" a cavernous room, square off an awkwardly long one. Strong colors seem to come at you; light colors go quietly into the distance. A coat of dark paint will visually bring down the ceiling and bring in the walls of a room. Dark end walls will make elongated space look square; bright slipcovers will enlarge a sofa or chair. Light colors work in reverse, since the eye accepts them without really seeing them. Therefore, light walls, ceiling and floor make a room look larger. So do unbroken sweeps of light

PASTELS = SOPHISTICATION
and elegance, in settings like this polished bedroom, where pink and white interplay to produce a femininity nicely lacking in froth. The only elaborate touch is the silky cord tassel swags added to the draperies and bedspread. Too often confined to the nursery (a double shame since babies love bright colors), pastels and the subtler, grayed shades create quiet rooms that inspire soft talk and relaxation.

PRIMARY COLORS = LIVELY ROOM

Broad sweeps of bold color would make this room feel modern even without its streamlined furnishings. Yellow and red, used right off the color wheel with no pacifiers added, literally vibrate the room to life, and demand action and animated talk from its inhabitants. Actually, the furnishings are classically simple despite their modernity—even the rug's almost oriental in design. Smashing primary colors create all the activity.

COLOR FLOWS, SPACE GROWS

Or so it seems to when there are no sharp contrasts to stop the eye. Yellow is ubiquitous in the bedroom above, blending floor, tables, bed canopy, spread and window (including its heating duct and shade) into one nice illusion of uncluttered space.

CAMOUFLAGE WITH PATTERN

Now you see it—now you don't doubt what legerdemain color and pattern can work. Wallpaper brings this derelict chest back into the family circle. But none too prominently, which is just why it's covered to blend, chameleon-like, into the wall. You can pull the same disappearing act with slipcovers to "stretch" this average room.

color. Paint woodwork, radiators, jumbled architectural details all the same hue, then hang draperies to match—instant space! On the other hand, you can add drama to a room by using bright color for deliberate contrast. Painted beams against a white ceiling are a classic example. Or one wall painted a surprise color that is picked up elsewhere in the room. Coordinate, camouflage, contrast—it can all be done with color.

But which ones?

After all our analysis and discussion, the answer is still the same—choose colors you like, colors that become you, colors you can live with and look at happily. Then, once you've decided you want a "blue" room, for example, you need a specific starting blue to build that room around, your heirloom Wedgwood, a carpet you already own, or—easiest—a print fabric with color harmonies already worked out for you by professional artists. You can simply lift their color schemes from the fabric and enlarge them to fit over your entire room, translating into paint, solid fabrics or coordinating prints as you go.

Here, too, there is a general formula to help you keep your colors and prints in pleasing proportions: subdivide your room into (1) Dominant areas—walls, floor, ceiling; (2) Medium areas—windows, large upholstered furniture, beds; (3) Accents—trimmings, pillows, accessories, etc.

Now start applying your colors, remembering that the dominant and medium areas will carry your scheme. Remember, too, that the larger the area, the softer the color should be unless you are intentionally seeking drama. A great way to deal with a really smashing color is to use it in a single broad sweep, on one wall or an area rug, for example, then repeat it in a throw pillow, tablecloth trimming, picture matting, etc. Never, never use a color just once; add a mini-touch of it here and there to show you meant it. And *don't* believe that all colors should be treated equally. Nothing's duller than two hues given equal time in a room. Let one dominate, the other play counterpoint.

At the same time, keep in mind the "weightiness" of color and pattern, and keep them well-balanced throughout the room, soothed, if need be, by generous helpings of the neutrals—white, black, grays and beiges. If you are translating your color scheme from a fabric, its background color might flow comfortably onto the dominant areas in your room. Then pick up an important second hue for the medium areas, and follow through with accents in its zestiest color. How and where to repeat the

COLOR CONTRASTS *can bring a room to life, even when the colors are as light as the yellow-white combination on the next page. Instead of glossing one color over both wall and woodwork, the latter is picked out with bright yellow. There's just enough contrast to add interest, but not so much that the room becomes busy and the beams seem lower. However, strongly contrasting colors can be used effectively where more drama is desirable.*

patterned fabric itself is a matter of good balance, since patterns look "heavier" than plain fabrics.

You may like the allover look, where a fairly quiet pattern flows from walls to windows to slipcovers, leaving solid colors to play the accent roles. Or you may hang patterned draperies, match them with several major slipcovers, then follow the distribution system above for walls, floor and other up-

holstered pieces. You can mix patterns, too, *if* you know the magic word for success—*contrast*. If they are unalike enough in pattern—e.g., a floral and a geometric—yet alike in color structure, two or even three patterns can find visual happiness together. So can two patterns that are alike in design, provided they differ greatly in scale. A large houndstooth and small check, a floral and a floral stripe, or a rectangular and a circular abstract can all work hand-

BUILDING
AROUND A PRINT

This is one of the surest ways to arrive at a pleasing color scheme. And the print need not always be a fabric, as proved by the room at left, where a prized oriental rug sets the pace. Its warm background tone flows onto the wall. Chairs, couch cover, facing for fireplace and cube tables pick up other colors. Accents echo the rug's brightest hue, which is also found in the drapery fabric.

Little things, like this pleasant collection of bright glass, can give a big boost along the way to a color scheme. Here, the colors of the collection are stretched over the entire dining area. The bright blue begot the rug and the table accents; the amber is found again in the chair seats and china; they are repeated along with the green in the richly printed wallpaper and matching slipcover fabric.

BUILDING
AROUND OBJECTS

BALANCING PATTERN

is a matter of playing it off against restful solid areas. This handsome room follows an almost infallible formula: patterned draperies are balanced by sofa, counterbalanced by chair seats. The fabric's background color flows onto walls. Molding, accessories and armchair pick up the bright yellow. Muted rug unites all colors.

somely, provided they have a common color denominator. And provided that here, again, you let one play the dominant role in the room. To use two patterns equally equals confusion.

It will aid your planning to know that the subtle patterns of damasks, brocades, sculptured rugs, etc., are usually treated as solid colors. Richly patterned oriental rugs fall into a unique category, too. They have always been at home with traditional patterns—stripes, geometrics and such—in period rooms, but let your eye be your guide with outspoken contemporary prints.

Now, you're equipped with a new understanding of the way colors react to each other, to light, to large and small areas. You've analyzed how you react to them, and you're armed with a sample color or fabric print from which you will build your color scheme. You're ready to decide just how you want to put that scheme together. There are various ways of combining colors in a room, of course, but the three most universally successful are built around monochromatic, complementary and related colors.

A fourth—and always dramatic—color scheme can be created from black-and-white *plus*...the plus is one other important color used as accent. Black-white-and-red have been worked together so often you'd think they'd become cliché, but somehow the trio almost always comes out looking fresh and zesty.

A bright, aggressive green looks great, too, against a black-and-white ground. In fact, almost any color can be the "plus" in a basically black-and-white room as long as it's strong enough to pull its own weight.

Enough *talk* of colors. Pictures really are worth thousands of words, so let's *look* at colors.

PLAYING UP PATTERN

pulls a room together and produces a subtle kind of decorating excitement in the process. Because this print is smallish and cool in shades of blue, it's calm enough to use in a bedroom. Actually, its overall-ness is comfortably enveloping—look how the room's one solid accent, the chair cushion, suddenly stands out! You can use fabric for both walls and covers, or, as here, select material that has wallpaper to match. Manufacturers have many such coordinates.

PATTERN
PERVADES

The print's charming, and especially practical in this one-room apartment, since it makes the most of minimum space. But to keep it from being overwhelmingly vigorous, woodwork and window blinds are painted black, three walls white, and rug is kept quiet underfoot.

PATTERN MIX

MIX *calls for two seemingly contrary qualities—contrast and compatibility. The contrast should come in size and pattern. Here, the tiny wallpaper print plays off nicely against the large rug pattern, and the geometrics on wall and floor live happily with the floral slipcovers. For compatibility, you need a common color denominator. Here, it's blue, braced with yellow and underscored by white (which always goes a long way to relieve the tensions that can arise when patterns are thrown into a potpourri).*

PATTERN MIX

can be a smash! or a mish-mash, if you don't let one dominate in a room setting. Five different patterns play across this Colonialesque bedroom (deliberately shown in black and white to point up the interplay of the prints). Yet the room succeeds because the other four patterns accede to the trellis design on walls, beds and windows.

ELEGANTLY SUBTLE

is the way to describe the total effect of a monochromatic color scheme. Done well, such a plan always comes out looking sophisticated and serene since there are no sharp color changes to jar the eye or psyche. Just choose the color you love most and play it up and down the scales, as the designer has done in the dining bay, left, where earth tones range from slate to putty to terra cotta, accented in snow white.

TEXTURIZE

Monochrome might mean monotony without a variety of textures to keep the eye occupied. There's plenty for visual interest in the all-pink bedroom at the right, from the smooth window shades to the crushed velvet on canopy and spread, the striations on the corner chair and, finally, the tousled shag carpet. Even the collection of glass paperweights introduces another, welcome texture—gleaming hardness—in a room that's soft on both eye and soul, despite its robustly basic warm color.

MONOCHROMATIC COLOR SCHEMES

THINK
NO-COLOR

and your thoughts may be as beautiful as this all-white drawing room, where only the sofa, in a reserved green velvet, and handsome old books break the color barrier . . . ever so decorously. Here, where texture is even more essential, the velvets work nicely against the gleaming tile floor; pleated lampshades, cane-backed chair and the natural touch of plants and bare branches are visually important. All-white — or no-color — schemes are also good in modern rooms.

ACTIVATE

Scientists may still be searching, but interior designers discovered the secret of life ages ago—it lies in complementary color schemes. Red and green, each just a little off-key, send a cacophony of color reverberating through this fun, sun porch, with only the white walls soft-pedaling. Obviously, the owners never meant it for quiet drowsing or they wouldn't have included so many activity areas—for conversation and games.

COMPLEMENTARY COLOR SCHEMES

THEY VIBRATE

And they prove that opposites do attract. Complementary colors lie opposite each other around the color wheel; they are the colors most unalike. Yet they can be quite attractive together when they are paired with care. See what happens to this quiet blue bedroom when just a soupçon of its complement, orange, is added.

REVERSE
ROLES

and the emphasis is on orange this time, with blue back-stepping into the accent role. This lively kitchen proves again the power of a complement. Color schemes based on them are visually, emotionally stimulating, therefore especially great in the active areas of a home—kitchen, playroom or sun porch, as we've just seen. But, as we've also just seen on the preceding page, complements can be tailored to suit even a bedroom.

RELATED COLOR SCHEMES

FAMILY TRAIT

of related colors, those found next to each other on the color wheel, is to get on harmoniously together. That's why rooms based around related colors are usually restful and refreshing. But not unexciting, as you can see from the spring-fresh bedroom, left, with its greens-and-yellow theme. In fact, the colors combine almost too smoothly, so black, the super-neutral, is added for crispness, in the print, in the fringe trimming and around the frame of the painting.

ONCE TABOO

together, for reasons no one seems to remember now, blue and green are two of the most compatible relatives on the color wheel. Certainly they've been two of the most popular in recent years. Here, in a room devoted almost entirely to them, blue and green pair off in an unusual window treatment. One long picture window lies behind that triple helping of draperies over sheer curtains. Plywood beams were added.

WARM FAMILY
feeling comes from the part of the color wheel that lies opposite the cool blue-green side. In the bedroom above, yellow runs into many of its orange relatives, then on to almost-red in the window screens, lamp shade and picture frame. Such paprika-and-saffron flavorings fit right in with the Spanish mood of the room, proving that not all related color schemes have to come out looking restful. It all depends on how you play the colors, which one is cast in the lead part.

QUIETER FAMILY
reunion results when the same slice of the color wheel — containing the yellow-orange relatives — is turned in a different direction, right. Yellow, toned up and down with white, has the lead role here, with orange staying politely in the background, never nearing the intensity it was allowed above. So this room is calm, despite its cheeriness. The same room can have many other moods, however, as shown on the next eight pages. It's color that makes the great difference.

YELLOW ACCENTS

this version of the
same room. Here it
is played against a
paled gray-green
background that in-
cludes walls, sofa
cover and the plaid
in the armless chairs.
In terms of territory,
yellow is secondary
but its natural bois-
terousness still
makes it the center
of attraction. Com-
pare this classic,
composed scene with
the all-yellow room
on the preceding
page—more proof of
how compatible re-
lated colors are.

SUPREMELY GREEN

This is truly a one-color room—the very same fresh green upholsters the chairs, covers sofa, windows and carpet, then runs across the ceiling with its arbor-like paper pattern. There is none of the variation in intensity that usually marks a monochromatic scheme. Instead, fresh, sparkling white—the un-color—becomes the alter ego that makes this room click.

OPENLY ORANGE

White to the rescue once again, saving this bright orange room from melting in its own warmth! The cool white walls, sheer curtains and accessories, plus the dark wood of the floors and furniture are the perfect foils for the intense glow orange imparts, especially when it's teamed with an equally exuberant relative on the color wheel, yellow.

FEELING BLUE

would be an enviable state if it manifested itself in a room like this. Richly monochromatic from the walls right down to the carefully chosen accessories, it allows only off-white as an interloper. But that and the variety of textures on carpet and slipcovers make it a visually stimulating room. And keep it from succumbing to the major drawback of blue—its inherent coldness.

COMPLETELY IN PINK

The same room and the same monochromatic approach to a color scheme. But the all-blue and rather worldly room on the preceding page here turns into a soft and very intimate retreat from the world and its aggressions. Pink is like that, psychologically sheltering, emotionally—and physically—flattering to those who dwell "in the pink" literally.

BLACK AND WHITE

Here comes a sampling of another, very exciting kind of color scheme—black-and-white plus one other vigorous color. Above, that color is red, run underfoot, around the sofa cover and onto the accessories. Black-and-white-and-red are the traditionally successful Big Three in this kind of decorating, but by no means do they have a monopoly, as the coming pages prove.

METALLIC

touch of chain, brass nail heads, lamp shade and furniture legs takes the place of color as the third member of the black-and-white-plus approach to the window treatment, left. Direct, simple and completely unfrilled, with Napoleonic overtones, it's the epitome of masculinity. Black-and-white-plus can also look elaborate, depending on the color company they keep.

BLACK-WHITE PLUS YELLOW

inspired by the large portrait, set the color theme for this inexpensively furnished apartment room. Its occupants invested most of their decorating money in the painting, but their bright, three-part color scheme was thrown in for free. Unfinished Parsons tables and cube were do-it-yourself projects, covered in self-sticking paper to carry out the black-white plan.

MANY 'PLUSES' HERE

Black and white still set the scene in the elegantly traditional living room, left, where they are used to dramatize the walls and woodwork. But there are many other color pluses at work to make the room come off looking so lush. Bright green is the major ally, underfoot in the plush carpeting and running through the print fabric at the windows and on the sofa. As this drawing room demonstrates, black-and-white need not be stereotyped into modern settings only. They're full of high drama, however, and must be skillfully handled in period rooms.

PRINTS PLUS RED

The sophisticated bedroom, below, captures the rules about using prints clearly in black and white (with their favorite companion, red, thrown in for verve). The contrast between curvilinear motifs on the wall and geometrics on bed and floor, plus the changes in scale, allow them to coexist dashingly. For more emphasis overhead, the soaring beams are painted black against the white ceiling, and the upward trend is continued in the fringed bed canopy. There's a final touch of black and white in the furniture, pillows, and on the opaque lamp shade.

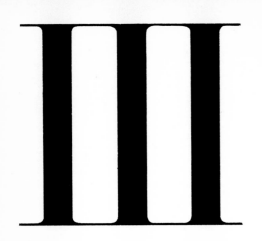

ROOMS ON VIEW

Good decorating is boundless…truly. All the ideas about taste and balance, color and coordination that apply to one room run right over the threshold and through the entire house. But how they are applied varies from room to room just as the focus and the function of each room varies. Since "form follows function" is a foremost decorating rule, it's important to analyze the purpose of each room to understand where the emphasis should lie so the room works as well as it looks. All kinds of rooms are reviewed in the following section. They are grouped according to their function, beginning with the entrance hall and leading through the whole house, but you won't find any clichés among them. The days when rooms were furnished according to formulae—e.g., dining room equals table, chairs, buffet and chandelier—have gone the way of matching furniture suites.

These days, anything goes anywhere it has a *raison d'etre*. You'll find wardrobes holding dishes in the dining room, hatracks dispensing towels in the bath. In decorating, as in many other areas of modern life, we're free from *de rigueur* rules, free to create our own natural habitat, to surround ourselves with what we like, to put it where we like...as long as all is done with good taste. Good taste may come in many guises, but it's never disguised. As you review the rooms that follow, you'll find it in the way furniture is arranged, the way colors are coordinated and windows dressed to serve a certain purpose.

These are rooms filled with 1,001 decorating ideas for you to analyze, enjoy and borrow—intact, if you like—for your own home. You'll find some bright new ways to look at every room under your roof, some clever solutions for nearly every decorating problem under the sun. But these ideas are really meant to inspire—to turn on your imagination so that you can create your own design for living.

MAKE A GRAND ENTRANCE

Your entrance hall has the first—and last—word when it comes to greeting guests. It should say "welcome" with real enthusiasm, "good-bye" with special warmth. And with a little coaxing, it can go on to tell a lot about the people who live in the home behind it . . . whether they're formal or casual, lovers of Early American, Modern or mixed. Entries are like appetizers: small, appropriate samples of the main course to come. And like appetizers, they should be kept simple. Most home and apartment builders have seen to it that they are kept small. But the welcome can be as big as the baronial-sized receiving halls of yesteryear's castles. This is the place for small, bright touches, beginning with a good lighting fixture so guests can see themselves coming and going. (When it's hung overhead, make sure it's well *over* heads.) An entry hall mirror is a doubly good idea, allowing last-minute check-ups and also enlarging the space. Small-scaled furniture also stretches space; so do wall-hung pieces that free the floor. Along with all the esthetics, don't neglect the practical purpose of an entrance hall: it's the place for shedding hats, coats and wet umbrellas, and for shaking off the mud and dust of the outdoors. Dress it accordingly in muss-resistant fabrics and flooring, so the "welcome" on your red carpet is easy to read.

Big drama in small quarters comes from making the most of these entry-way walls. Arches are cut from paisley vinyl fabric and glued to painted blue background. Edging of white braid adds to the illusion of depth. Chain-hung lacquer shelf acts as a catchall without sacrificing space on the floor, an echo of the wall.

Hall of mirrors! Actually the shimmering entry hall at left has only a mirror-paneled door and a Venetian mirror on the wall. The gleam and sparkle, however, are everywhere...reflected by the crystal accessories, the silver wall coverings, and the metalized woodwork. (Mirrors are ideal for any small room because they make it look larger.) Note super checks on floor.

Early American puts a charming face forward in the foyer above, created in a once-characterless space by painted plank walls and the brick-patterned floor. All the accessories are carefully chosen to carry on the theme, but the entrance hall has its practical features too: umbrella stand, clock, shelf and deacon's bench make it more than just a passing affair.

Warm welcome in the cheery hallway, left, comes from the warm yellow-orange color scheme that has been kindled in the formerly plain-white area. Sparked by the rug, foyer's done with paint (on the paneled door) and with ordinary burlap, trimmed with braid (used for the tied-back draperies and wide valance with recessed lighting).

Behind many big-city apartment doors lurks an uninspiring entry-way niche like this one used to be. Instead of walking right past it, the residents here have capitalized on the awkward jut in the corner, matching it with a panel that divides the handy storage cabinets. Braid trimming and brightly striped flooring help change its anonymity to personality.

A dd a view to even the innermost entry-way. All it takes is an enlargement of a favorite landscape, framed in a homemade "window." The scene above was photostated and mounted on cardboard under a frame of 2 by 4s attached to the top of the chest. It is covered with a cane design to complement the airy bamboo wall covering. Sheer curtains and light chairs aid open effect.

P ièce de résistance comes right at the beginning of this handsome San Francisco town house, right. Large 18th-century Swedish stove dominates the entrance hall but doesn't overwhelm incoming visitors, thanks to the light, open colors and spare use of accessories. They've been mounted on the wall to carry the eye up and leave the floor to traffic, plants and a pair of useful side chairs.

An oversized guest closet turned inside-out to open up a whole new useful life for this entry-way-cum-home office. The clever designer took off the center doors of the closet, removed the clothes rack and added shelves instead. Fabricked doors and glued-on beams, painted white, give character to this once typically dull apartment entrance.

Here's a foyer idea that's as handsome as antique tiles and as easy as rolling off a few yards of self-adhesive paper. The paper comes down part of the wall, runs over the cantilevered shelf and onto the unwalked-upon part of the floor. The area rug absorbs most traffic, making the paper floor practical even in a heavily traveled entry-way.

LIVING ROOMS

What's in a name? Call it the drawing room, front room or parlor, but still the living room is the room for family *living*. Even when a recreation room relieves it of day-to-day heavy duty, the living room is important as the official gathering spot, the room that represents the family to friends and visitors. Therefore, it's the room that comes first to most minds when it comes to decorating, the room that receives the greatest share of time, attention and allotment from the budget. It's also the room that causes the greatest share of head-aches, simply because it contains the most flexible space in the entire house. Dining rooms just naturally call for furniture to dine from, bedrooms require beds, etc. But living rooms are wide open spaces that can be filled with any manner of furnishings, given many different personalities. It all depends on the family that lives therein and the way they live—formally, with damasks and antiques, or comfortably with TV and corduroy covers. Analyze your Family Personality and the role your living room will play in your home—e.g., showplace or activity area. Decide what kind of furniture you need to make it fill that role. Lots of seating? A desk, book storage, dining area? Only when you've settled such essentials, are you ready to create a *look* for your living room.

The rustic living room on the opposite page had an interesting personality to begin with, since it began life as a barn in Bucks County, Pennsylvania. But its renovators rightfully decided it needed a center of interest and added the dramatic two-story fireplace hood which soars the entire height of the living room, serving, in the process, to warm the balcony bedrooms which overlook the living area below.

Oriental rug inspired the unusual color scheme for the warm living room above. The rich chocolate from the rug design is used for walls, providing a soft foil for the bold cerise red accents inside the book cabinets which flank the sofa. The units also add some architectural interest to the otherwise squarish room.

Also opting for architectural interest where there was little naturally endowed, the living room below turns its back on its window wall. The view was drab anyway, much less interesting than the way the window looks now. The plywood panels, with their painted dado and "molding" made from gimp, can be rearranged.

Room with a smashing view—of the San Francisco harbor—is kept open and airy to take full advantage of its vantage point. But that doesn't mean the furnishings are without interest. On the contrary, the room is rich with pattern, texture and contrasts, between the unembellished architecture and the admixture of antiques: French chairs, Chinese coffee table, rare Samarkand rugs.

New angle gives a very new look to an ordinary, rectangular living room. Super-graphics, snaking up the wall and across the ceiling, is achieved with wide woven braid, glued in place. With this single inspired stroke, the walls become an important accessory to the contemporary mood of the room. And the angular design plays nice counterpoint to the opulent curves of the sofa, chair and lamps. The same idea could be executed with paint and rollers.

Texture is the thing that creates interest in the sophisticated living room at the left. All blond and silver, it takes warmth from the wood paneling, a bit of cold gleam from the stainless steel fireplace hood and strips which face the windows. Plants provide the only color in the room, which has off-white upholstery and shades, even on the lamp. But the overall effect, thanks to the varied textures, is richly eye-filling and elegant, in every modern sense.

Rich with tradition, yet light, bright and very livable, this living room shows "modern" colonial at its best. The furnishings are all good reproductions and there are none of the too-folksy touches that can undermine Early American rooms. Instead, the room has classic simplicity despite the vigorous colors in the fabric (which inspired the blue-white color scheme with its brief touches of red). Medallions from the fabric are used to trim valances and pillow.

Flamenco red and saffron give this living room its warm Spanish
flavoring. The furniture is basically any-style. With other upholstery, it could have gone easily into an entirely different setting.
However, when it's coordinated with color and backed with the right accessories—the brick tile floor, giant candlestick and draperies with their
jumbo ball fringe—it assumes its Mediterranean mood like a native.

Dining area can coexist happily with the rest of the living room as long as it's made to look welcome, planned for, not simply allowed to fill the corner most convenient to the kitchen. Here, the dining area is given its own identity, set off from the living room with added-on beams to mark the break. But it shares the same walls, floor and color scheme, carried out on draperies, cushions and renovated wardrobe.

Living room for lovers of things unusual is a treasure trove of originality. Old iron fireplace is Dutch, lamps flanking it are made from English water filters. An umbrella rack now does duty as the bar, and fiber placemats are framed to conceal a corner window. Chairs are covered in wide braid, studded to match the rachet-arm sofa and antique leather chest. There's even modern Plexiglas in the game table. For all its whimsy, the room works well and is as functional as it is fun.

City Mix—a sophisticated blend of furnishings from many moods, many periods—describes all three rooms on this page. Above, the blend tends to look traditional, although its major furnishings are basically modern. Accessories and color set the mood.

The room at the right is close kin to the one above. They share a similar color scheme and mostly modern furnishings. But mood-wise, they're on opposite sides of the City Mix family. This is a brighter, gayer, of-the-moment room. Again, credit the accessories.

A man who likes anything good, regardless of its chronology, has created comfortable City Mix in his New York City townhouse, left. Living together beautifully: French-flavored hanging shelf, antiques like the coal scuttle, modern and provincial pieces.

Modern with an air of traditional good breeding — this living room is almost all angles, all up-to-date ideas. But even a classicist could live here happily, lulled by the textured upholstery fabrics in herringbone and velvet, and by the rich veneers on the rosewood trophy cabinets and small chest. Overall, the room has a classic calm, despite its sparsity of line and "hard edge" chrome legs on desk, chair.

Architecturally treated window and wall paneled in plain crate wood painted white create an understated but interesting background in the living room at left. Colors are kept fresh and sunny, even underfoot where textured tile replaces dark flooring. Lambrequin around the window is not difficult to make from plywood.

Fluid space flows as freely as all outdoors through the room above. And since the outdoors is a magnificent setting near Seattle, the indoors is quietly underplayed with soft colors and natural materials to let the scenery preside. The eye is carried right through the glass doors onto the deck by the steel beams and unusual ceiling.

O pen-air window wall willed this living room into its fresh, informal look. Windows are allowed to steal the scene since they show off gardens both outside and inside, where a planter border is made with pebbles. Simple roman shades that pull up for maximum sunshine are set in a wooden frame outlined with red braid that ties them all together in one bright bracket. The braid also picks up the red flower in the slipcover fabric and appears again on the armchair.

DINING ROOMS

Don't take the "room" too literally. Anywhere you dine can be a dining room, whether it's a niche in the living room or a wide apartment foyer. We've come through that inelegant era when the dining room was ignored and eating became a kind of kitchen-counter affair. It was a matter of merely eating, too. To truly *dine* requires a gracious setting, an appetizing atmosphere no matter where it's located. Color can help you create that atmosphere, soft colors that soothe like candlelight, or, conversely, bright red that stimulates the appetite. Physical comfort is another consideration. Be sure chairs are sitable and suitably pitched, the table big enough to allow generous elbow room, serving counters convenient, and undertable rugs sufficiently large for push-back room without chair legs stepping off. Mood lighting is especially important in the dining area. You need only enough to see by easily, so keep lights soft, bulbs small. Consider installing a dimmer that lets you adjust the light level to suit the occasion. Choose a chandelier styled to match the mood of the room, and be sure it looks big enough when hung—well above the heads of diners (30-to-36 inches over the table). Though chandeliers are dining room standards, look to wall sconces, lamps, even real candles as a way around the ordinary. In fact, why serve any clichés at all?

Mood of old Mexico materializes in modern dining room, thanks to today's technology. Beams overhead are light-weight fiber glass; flooring underfoot is easy-care vinyl emulating authentic Mexican tile; hardboard filigree panels pose as window grillwork; "carved" door is done with glued-on fringe. Furniture, accessories are authentic, however.

Convivial and conducive to after-dinner talks, the dining room above is warmly Mediterranean with its Spanish accent pieces and richly patterned red window dress. Elaborate, shaped valance, tasseled to match the high tie-backs, is cut from plywood and covered with fabric carefully positioned to show off the medallion motif. Braid trimming on curtains echoes the Spanish rug fringe.

Checked fabric, run freely over walls, French doors and tassel-tie chair cushions, makes the dining room at the right pleasantly provincial. Woodwork and beams are painted the same antique shade of blue as the table and large cupboard, both contemporary reproductions of country-made furniture from yesteryear. Just for fun, matching scraps of the print are fringed for informal placemats.

Colonial Williamsburg, beautifully restored and furnished with elegant 18th-century antiques, epitomizes the look most traditionalists love—subtle elegance, rich fabrics, softened colors for walls and woodwork. Dining in Old Virginia was a formal affair, at least for the George Wythe family, in whose home the room at left was photographed. The Wythes enjoyed their Smithfield ham and Sally Lunn bread in polished splendor.

Here, the same formal feeling is recaptured in modern-made "antiques." Chairs, table, sideboard and chandelier are available for anyone who, like the Wythes, wants mealtimes to be lovely times. The styles aren't copied exactly from Colonial Williamsburg, but the mood is maintained with softly painted paneled walls and fringed draperies in the background, polished brass overhead and lush oriental carpeting on the floor under the dining group.

Window shade and fabric-covered screens set the dining room above with tailored simplicity. Gold is the only color allowed, used on the wall-to-wall carpeting and in the wall stripes that are the only decoration. Stripes are strips of wide woven braid, which also edge the screens and shade, then make loops to hold the brass rod used to raise and lower it. The clean-lined Scandinavian style furnishings are good choices for the setting.

Equally streamlined, and modern from its twinkling ceiling to the dramatic tile floor, the room at the right has a special kind of glow. The luminous wall is achieved with fluorescent fixtures hidden behind panels of stretched fabric. The light diffuses softly and interestingly into the area, which would be dark and boxy otherwise. The floating glass shelf and lithe-legged furniture also add to the illusion of overall lightness.

Ingenuity more than equals good architectural endowment in this dining room with its look of year-round Spring. There's no view at all behind that window. But the airy trellis and lightweight draperies achieve a feeling of openness, aided and abetted by the glass and wrought-iron garden furniture, and by the vinyl flooring. It brightly repeats the flower colors from the drapery fabric. More ingenuity: trellis is made of carpet tape stapled to a plywood frame.

Ideas are featured on the bill of fare for the dining room opposite. Little original touches bring the room to life: window swags with jabots lined to match the green in the stenciled floor, for example, and the collection of brass candlesticks on the mantle, clustered to balance the painting. Even it is hung interestingly off-center.

Old World emphasis on ceilings inspired the apartment owner to scale a ladder and set to work on his own dining room, above. The elaborate "moldings" are effected with paint and furniture gimp. More sumptuousness comes from fabric-covered walls, ceiling-hung draperies and the layered table skirt, lined to match chairs.

Daisy fresh—even the old expression takes on fresh meaning in the dining room at the left. Flowers bloom from floor to ceiling, in ceramic tiles, fringe and even on the painted furniture. Tile and trim find new roles as door framing and ceiling molding, respectively. The checked fabric used throughout the room is reversible—it literally turns inside-out to add variety to walls, French doors, table and chair cushions. A sleeve of fabric also dresses the chain on the matching green-and-white light.

Traditional linen print suits the mood of the rambling old fourteen-room farmhouse where this dining room is located. But the print's applied in a pleasant new way for more than conventional interest around the dado. With the Gibraltar-like radiator under the windows, only single drapery panels could be used at the sides. But the pleated valance carries the print right up to ceiling level. In its secluded setting, no further window covering is needed, but solid shades would solve any privacy problem.

*F*ireplace flanked by lovely long windows presents a setting that takes some living up to, decoratively speaking. This dining room does, thanks, in large part, to the handsome blue and white floral stripe fabric. Used with a lavish hand, it covers the shaped cornices over tied-back draperies, then runs over the walls. Dark blue velvet is used to outline the window treatment, providing nice counterpoint for the painted beams overhead. Because the windows are so generous in this city setting, short cafes prevent a too-bare look.

THE KITCHEN STORY

There was a time when the kitchen wasn't even allowed in the house. During Colonial days, it was often exiled across the backyard or held at a respectful distance by a breezeway. Then servants went out and kitchens came back in to become the warm heart of most homes, the hub around which family life revolves at least three times a day. Today's kitchens are pleasant places to be, for both cooks and kibitzers. We've lost our mania for antiseptic appearance in appliances. Refrigerators, stoves—nearly everything, *including* the kitchen sink—now come in decorator colors and styles to compete with any room in the house. Washable papers make pretty walls practical. Wall-to-wall carpeting's in the kitchen now. Pots, pans and everyday dishes have gone high style. Even workaday linens drop designer names once reserved for the world of *haute couture. Haute cuisine* now reigns supreme—scrambled eggs end up as soufflés, fondue is a household word, and almost everyone can create an uncurdled hollandaise. Did kitchens inspire the current interest in cooking, or was it the other way around? No matter, for even those who'd blanch at a *toque blanche* can enjoy living in today's plug-in, push-button, turned-on environment. As the succeeding pages will prove, there's almost no end to the kinds of kitchens you can cook up.

*T*urn back the hour glass—here's a modern kitchen with a charming chimney corner that could have been borrowed right from a Colonial American cook house. Art, wallpaper and accessories carry on the homespun feeling. Designed for cook-ins as well as atmosphere, the chimney's centered in this large kitchen so both working and eating areas face it.

Some hae meat that canna eat
And some wad eat that want it
But we hae meat and we can eat
Sae let the Lord be thankit.

Underground elegance surfaced when an imaginative young stage set designer went to work on this basement kitchen in Greenwich Village. The 135-year-old storage building he turned into a handsome home has only one room on each of its four floors, so basement serves for both dining (above) and cooking (shown left).

Rough old stone walls and timbers which had been buried behind crude paneling now provide the perfect setting for the 18th-century Spanish table and chairs. Carved cabinets with work-surface tops do double fix-and-serve duty. Downlights were added among the beams to illuminate without lowering the ceiling.

Country French fla-
vors the dining
area, then runs
down the tiled floor
through the kitchen.
Checked curtains and
dark-stained wood car-
ry the continuity be-
tween the rooms. The
kitchen features a free-
standing work counter
in its center over which
hangs the hallmark of
French kitchens, a pan
rack rich with copper
cooking gear. Walls are
cork above tile area.

*W*all-to-wall scenery was too good to cover with kitchen cabinets in the Washington State home, above. So the designer simply hung them from the ceiling and arranged access from both sides. Now they serve both the kitchen and the breakfast room.

*S*unny Mediterranean clime is created in the kitchen, opposite, with warm oranges and the right accessories. In fact, the design of the resilient tile floor is adapted from the old tile floors in the town hall of Barcelona. Moorish arches inspired the unusual window treatment. The chairs are Spanish imports and the copperware is antique.

Architectural interest you buy in a can and by the foot turns plain-Jane kitchen into the entertaining area above: ordinary walls were brushed with textured "stucco" paint, then the polyurethane beams were adhered on top. Plants thrive in the window sun, so shade is more attractive than essential. Cabinets are fabricked to match.

Full of vitamin C, the kitchen on the next page radiates citrus colors picked up from the wallpaper. Shaped plywood window valances are covered with paper to match, then trimmed with glued-on bands of gimp. More gimp accents the shades and cafes. Charcoal gray cabinets, white tabletop add a note of calmness.

In very Early America, the kitchen comprised the entire house since most log cabins were only one large room. The fireplace served as stove, furnace and source of light, so life truly centered around the hearth—as it does in these two modern kitchens. But the one at left wears a very 20th-century face—"stones" are actually molded fiber glass panels. So is the "barnwood" on cabinets, walls.

Cozy corner for family dining features a raised brick fireplace on one wall and a good view at the other when the cafe curtains are drawn aside. Their ball fringe trimming, repeated on the table cover, is appropriate in the informal, Early American setting. So are the documentary wallpaper and hanging copper lamp. Cabinet set into the wall between fireplace and window is an old country piece.

R ed, white and black—not quite Early America's true colors, but truly attractive in this Early American kitchen (below) with its around-the-counter breakfast area (right). In fact, the vinyl-coated wallpaper is crisply modern. Still, it coexists cheerfully with such antique touches as the rug, lamp and sleigh seat.

S lick patent-like red vinyl backs the spatter area behind the stove and adds bright touch to the cabinets' knotty pine quaintness (below). Same wall and window treatments, featuring scalloped roman shades striped with carpet tape, is carried over from the dining area.

T iny kitchen corner proves that little things can indeed mean a lot. Tucked into a New York City high-rise, the breakfast area opposite is mini, its effect mighty because the interior designer who lives there threw away that maxim about keeping small spaces plain.

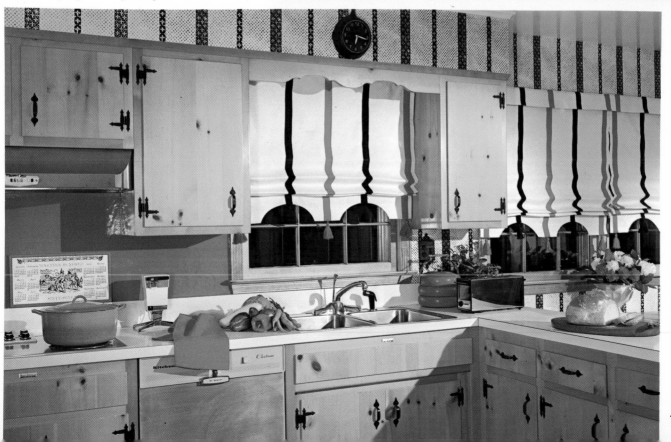

Full of the promise of fun, the family room above is comfortable, cheerful and easy to keep. The warm plaid rug sets both the room's playful mood and its bright color scheme, which is repeated on the sculptured seats and around the felt-covered walls. Plywood panels, wrapped in felt, trim the walls and divider screen, adding visual interest color-keyed to the carpet. Strictly for fun: plastic sculptured balls and game tables.

FAMILY ROOMS

One of the nicest ideas to materialize in the Twentieth Century, family rooms aren't completely new. Homes used to have libraries, music rooms, back parlors, etc.—all areas where family members could relax and pursue their own activities away from the polished company parts of the house. Furnishings were less formal and the neatness regimen a little more lax, but it wasn't until the Twentieth Century and its great change in life style that the family room could really evolve. Other names by which it is known—*rumpus* room and *recreation* room, for example—sum up those changes. Today we let the living room keep its coat and tie on in case company comes calling. But we need a shirtsleeves kind of room, too, a room where the family can let its hair down and put its feet up, where the children can lie upside-down to watch television and eating is more than allowed. This is not to define family rooms as *rumpled* or *wreck* rooms, however. Modern technology lets us have our cake and eat it, too, without worrying over stains on the carpet or upholstery. Family rooms can and should be as muss-proof as today's home furnishings will allow. Resilient floors, indestructibly engineered carpeting, plastic upholstery that can look as elegant as brocade or suede yet whisk clean with soap and water—all these belong in family rooms. Plan for fun-without-fuss. And make the room itself a fun place, with a sense of humor, a snappy color scheme, some secret whimsy reserved just for family and good friends.

No British colonist ever took tea in a breezier setting than this light-hearted family room. Brick tiles on floor and wall, shutters, plants and wicker furniture lend outdoors-like appeal. There's humor in the hanging pompons and stern ancestor portrait, thrift in the covered plywood cubes.

A real bargain basement discovery, the Early American family room on the opposite page makes good use of once unloved basement space. The only hint of its underground location now is in the small windows—there's glass only behind the curtained part on top. Illusion-makers below are still-life prints mounted against the paneled wall and framed to make the window space seem more generous.

Another space that led a relatively useless life, this spare bedroom has been upbraided, literally — and inexpensively—into a bright family room. Braid is woven in to customize the blind, used again to "cane" a repainted, castoff chest, and glued down the fronts of the added-on wall beams. Crossed with shelving and laced with curtain rods, those beams make a novel magazine rack.

F*ranklin stove, delightfully reproduced and available today, offers a quaint variation on the fireplace so many people insist upon. The brick chimney backing is both attractive and practical when the stove's roaring away. Equally attractive and practical: hardboard wall paneling, adjustable wall units, vinyl flooring. The table stands next to the kitchen for casual family meals. Unseen glass doors (at right) open to terrace.*

Shades of those trophy rooms from earlier eras, this family room leans toward the exotic. Zebra skin is real, but leopard spots on screen and chair were bagged in the decorating department (which features many wallpapers with fabrics to match). Two easy-care notables: vinyl upholstery and flooring.

Family room with the fringe on top offers an activity area for everyone ... all at the same time, too, thanks to its carefully planned, uncluttered arrangement. There's room for sitting, knitting, games, painting, reading or relaxing, plus a food supply center.

Red and wood warm up this Early American family room almost as much as the antique Franklin stove behind the table. Look again at that table —it's a very modern Parsons. Also modern and at ease in this decor: the vinyl floor posing as brick to underscore the homey theme. The room is actually built into a basement, but sleight of hand with light oak paneling and angled beams easily disguises that fact.

ere was one lovely way to get away from it all in the 18th Century. Photographed in Colonial Williamsburg, this bedroom would be a handsome retreat in any era, with its simple elegance. Colors are cool blue and white, but there's a pleasantly modern mixture of patterns—stripes on the bed and windows, print on the imported wallpaper. Chairs and table were for writing and reading.

MASTER BEDROOMS

A bedroom should be a bastion, a haven, a place for dreaming in every sense of the word. Make it soft and soothing, a sequestered retreat from the rest of the household world. At the same time, make it a round-the-clock room, useful beyond a mere eight hours at night. The right furnishings can stretch it into a place for personal activities—reading, letter-writing, sessions with the stereo . . . whatever interests the individuals whose room it is. For a bedroom, more than any other under the roof, is an individual room. It is here that personal preferences and prejudices (including a husband's) should be indulged, so the room truly reflects those who dwell within. Bedrooms always have, all through history. The status-conscious Egyptians first raised beds off the floor; the higher in the hierarchy, the higher the bed. Ancient Greeks so loved their beds that they stayed in them for meals, too. By the French Renaissance, bedrooms had become semipublic places, at least for royalty, who often held court among the comforts. Modern ideas about bedrooms have swung back to privacy and relaxation, goals that can be achieved with many different decors.

You'd have to get up pretty early in the morning to find a fresher approach to a bedroom. Bright and breezy with blues and greens setting a vibrant color scheme, the room comes off with a tropical air. Trace it to the "brass" bed (actually, gilt-finished wood), the live plants and windows treated simply with roman shades set behind a shaped plywood lambrequin.

*S*panish very definitely spoken here! From its tile patterned floor to the elaborately carved furniture and wrought iron, the bedroom at the right has a strong Spanish accent. It's a room with a masculine feeling, despite the dense fringe and swagged canopy.

*B*edroom for a Francophile, below, is heavily weighted toward antiques but light and airy in mood. Louis XVI bed upholstered in antiqued leather still has original white paint on the wood. An 18th-century French escritoire stands majestically by the window.

*I*talian emphasis on ceilings is interpreted in trimmings, right. Delicate braid outlines the arch into which the bed is recessed. A second, deeper niche neatly becomes a "bedside table," fabricked to match the bedspread. Wider braid trims window valance and pillow.

*C*ozily colonial bedroom below is bright with white furniture and jumbo ball fringe edging on the curved bed canopy and unusual window awnings. Fabric at the window repeats bed skirt, pillows and canopy lining. Double helping of shutters contributes to uncluttered effect.

Wall-to-wall fabric imparts a kind of restful drama to this French-flavored bedroom. The fabric, a handsome, 18th-century toile de Jouy, flows over onto the furniture, including the small table you have to look twice to see. In true period fashion, the bed is set into a niche, secluded behind draperies and a shaped valance.

143

*T*he provinces are revisited in the pleasantly informal bedroom above. Country and comfortable from its beams to plaid fabric, it has all the attributes of a real retreat, including frosted windows and a fireplace for warming the tea to be served on the curvy little table. Too much attention to period touches can make a room museum-like, but this one escapes by its livability.

*M*any things go to bring off the noncomformist room at the left as an interesting admixture of styles that may span centuries but never leave a gap in good taste. Period French chair and accessories coexist peacefully with super-modern pedestals, metal table and bed. Its simple, taut canopy of rough linen works well with the stucco walls, rough-hewn beams and matchstick blinds.

*S*pain reigns above in the repeated fringe trim, carved headboard, and leather touches on floor and wrought-iron stool. The bed curtains are miniature repeats of the windows, hung on a matching brass rod that has been cut in half and set into the wall. Although the Spanish look is usually massive and masculine, copious white touches keep this bedroom light, bright and open.

Classic case of elegance: marble floors and fireplace, paneled walls inset with rich wallpaper and, overall, a color scheme with the glow of old gold. Velvet is the obvious choice for fabrics, in the spread, on the open-arm wing chair and tied back at the windows. Accessories carry out the classic look.

Point-counterpoint, played out in plain and patterned fabric, makes the bedroom at right an agreeably lively place to be. Solid blue lines the bed canopy and window draperies, then skirts the round table. Plain areas on rug, dado also offset the pervasive pattern.

O
pposites do attract and ultimately
end up sharing the master bedroom. How, then, to let the room
reflect the tastes of both occupants if
she loves traditional and he insists on
streamlined modern? The twain meet
marvelously in this best-of-both-worlds
bedroom. On her side: candlewick
spread, Oriental rug, Delft-like drapery fabric with companion wallpaper.
Catering to him: hard-edged furniture, leather and steel chair, plain
fireplace wall painted solid.

Another happy marriage of ideas, this time about colors. She had her preference for pink and allover pattern; he wanted a masculine, brown bedroom, well-braced with dark woods. Since they both agreed on Early American, the rest came easily from the traditional print wallpaper with fabric to match. Double rows of ball fringe pick up the pink and brown.

CHILDREN'S ROOMS

Just as much as grown-ups, children deserve a retreat, a room where they can get away with their special thoughts, their friends, even their homework. "A room of my own," even when it's shared with siblings, is a cherished part of any child's life. In it tots can run and paint and play—he can slay dragons; she can raise her family of dolls. And teens can entertain—both friends and their own private thoughts. Carefully planned and furnished, the same room can grow right along with the child, practically from nursery school to college. There are cribs that convert to couches, desks you can expand into entire wall units, bunk beds that can go their separate ways as the need arises. Be practical about everything that goes into a youngster's room. Even for little girls, this isn't the place for touch-me-not furnishings. Floors and floor-coverings should be mar-proof or easily cleanable. Look for furniture with plastic-laminated tops, washable walls, fabrics that resist stains. Include plenty of room for storage, beginning with reachable hangers in the closet. Bulletin-board walls, toy chests, bookshelves, record racks are essential for neat keeping of the paraphernalia that make up every child's world. All this practicality isn't achieved at the expense of imagination, however. Decorating a child's room can be a great delight. Let your imagination romp. Choose a fanciful theme, create an environment that's bright and colorful, exciting and stimulating for the youngster who lives, plays, works and grows there.

Most ladylike room on the block, this young girl's retreat is all swags, gathers and tassels in feminine shades of lavender and white. The Austrian curtain at the window is repeated around the spread and across the plywood canopy. Not nearly as elaborate as it looks, the gathers can be let out flat on laundry day for easy washing and ironing.

Live! proclaims this colorful room. And a lively environment it is for a sophisticated girl teen of Today. There's not a trace of old-fashioned fluffiness: windows wear tailored shutters; bed, a sleek spread; floor, crisp black and white tiles. But for all its straight-forwardness, the room's still feminine, with bold color, patterns and personal touches like the painting above the bed.

Small room with seaworthy theme is so ship-shape, mates can bunk together without getting in each other's deck area. Beds cover storage drawers. Between them is a divider homemade of curtain rods and chain set into a wood frame. Matching wallpaper and fabric visually expand the limited space.

This is a room for a young man of any age, thanks to the cleanly styled furniture and simple, masculine window treatment. Rows of wide jute braid, mitered and tasseled at the ends, form a window frame and border the bright shades beneath. Trundle bed's ready for overnight guests.

For a cabin that's sure to buoy a boy's spirit, chart a nautical course to decorating. Hoist up the red, white and blue, add life preservers and section of wallpaper with seagoing theme, framed in double rows of cording. Frame is repeated at the window, where international signal flags spell out occupant's initials.

Splitting heirs, vertically, this double room uses bunk beds to clear as much floor space as possible. Built-in storage around the wall lets each boy enjoy his own desk space (carefully planned so their backs are to each other during homework sessions). Again, matching fabric and paper stretch space.

Any young Alice could make herself at home in this wonderland of a room. Based on fabric charmingly printed with Lewis Carroll's characters, it can grow and grow and grow with its occupant into her almost-teen years—there's an already-sophisticated touch in the dark-painted beams and bedhead, repeated by the chocolate ball fringe on curtains, canopy and lamp shade. Dresser and looking glass also have an ageless quality.

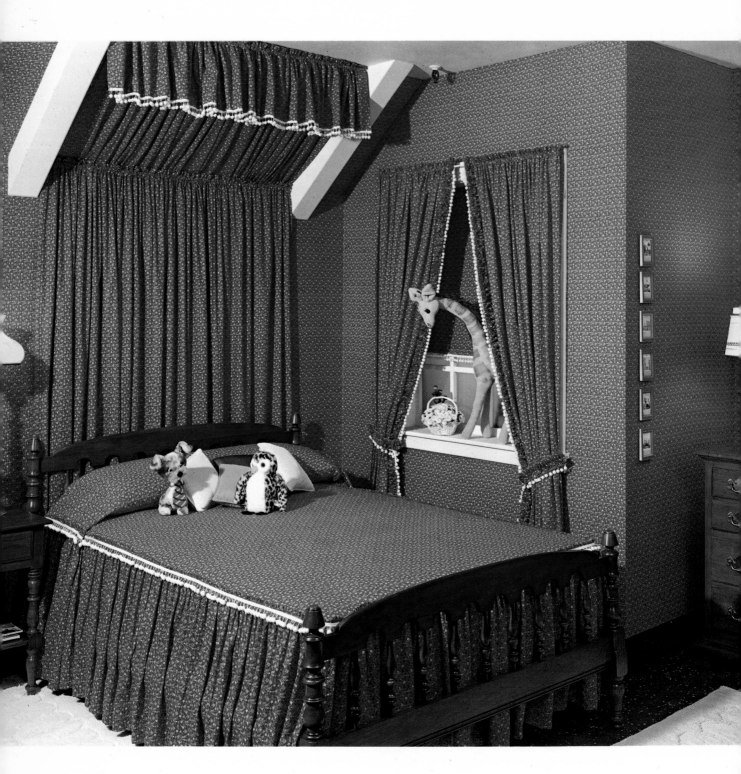

T ake two rooms tucked up under the eaves and add a perky print. Presto—
two rooms well worth the climb! An inexpensive calico, lavished upon
bed, walls and window, above, gives the small room a warmly furnished
look without actually filling the limited space. Dormer angle is emphasized
with white-painted beams, cut to fit. Canopy curtain is shirred on two rods.

Bouncy green and orange fabric lines the angled attic niche into which this bed is set, creating the feeling of a canopy. More of the print is used to cover the bed, back the unusual bench, and run up and over the window. The window canopy is shaped to repeat the curves of the charmingly colonial furniture, which was inspired by early Pennsylvania Dutch painted pieces.

Babies respond to bright colors and bold prints. What a shame they're so often stereotyped into living with pallid pastels and timid patterns! Bold red and white enliven this nursery (even in a black-and-white photograph). Much of the fun comes from the circus fabric used as canopies.

Room to grow in is pre-schooler pretty with ruffles and bows on bed, canopies and curtains. The painted furniture, here grouped for storage of toys, will still look timely as the tot grows to her teens and turns in the little-girl frills on the bed and at the window for more sophisticated treatments.

Lion's share of planning went into this colorfully coordinated circus room. The scallops on and over the bed and at the window are trimmed with two sizes of ball fringe. Leo himself is created from rows of rug fringe sewn to a pillow, then given gimp features. Note storage space and small work area.

*S*itting room fit for a teen is slick with vinyl valances and studio bed covers, and bright with stylized daisies on the dust ruffles and roman shades. Tailored for talk-sessions—the vinyls are almost lounge-proof—the room includes lots of pillows and tables for the inevitable snacks. The second bed's for overnight talk-ins. There's a study area, too, unseen at left.

S mall room gets a lot of flower power from one pretty print in wallpaper and matching fabric, used over windows, down wall and onto the bolsters and cover for the clever storage bed. The colors in the paper are picked up in the triple row of ball fringe on shades and cornices, then again for the solid colored rug, pillows and other furniture.

Even the allowance of the pre-teen who lives here could cover the cost of the fabric so grandly used for curtains, spread and cushions atop the chests-turned-window seats. It's plain cotton, about $1 a yard but made to look priceless with double rows of ball fringe. Note plywood window valance, cut to match the storage pieces by windows.

DENS AND GUEST ROOMS

Once upon more expansive times, every home had its guest room, a spare bedroom reserved just for visitors. Times have changed, houses have shrunk, and most "guest rooms" today must do double duty. They work for the family during the week—most often as dens—then convert to their hospitable roles with the ring of the doorbell. This needn't mean that guests must cope with less comfortable or convenient quarters. If the room's two lives are well-planned in advance, it can serve both purposes with equal grace. This usually means a comfortable bed that spends most of its time looking like a studio couch or tailored lounge. A headless, footless hollywood bed, covered with a trim spread and backed with wedges or bolsters, is always a good answer. So, of course, is a convertible sofa. Bedside tables and lamps, storage pieces and chairs should be selected with both den and bedroom use in mind. And remember when you dress windows that guests will require privacy and, perhaps, protection from early-morning glare. Try to keep one closet and a few drawers fairly clear, and to provide convenient space for suitcases. All this *can* be accomplished without sacrificing the way the room looks in either of its guises. The quartet of den-guest rooms coming up will prove that point attractively.

Here the bed is obviously a bed, but it doesn't disturb the library-like quality of this den-guest room. Handsome old furnishings, like the campaign desk, leather bookbindings and chair, are dignified against the giant paisley print wallpaper. With guests in mind, the strap draperies are lined against the light, and stool stands ready for suitcases.

Bachelor's study is all gleam and polish, with hard-edge furnishings and no-nonsense pieces like the very functional three-way lamp. Cool steel strips are set into the wall to reflect the metal touches on the lamp and tables. The room disdains coziness, but, with the rich woods and chaise upholstered in "heat waves," it's far from uncomfortable for overnight guests.

Despite its whimsical charm, this is the business end of a very versatile room that serves both family and visiting friends (an unseen sofa bed opens for instant hospitality). One unit along the wall houses books, stereo equipment and music library, plus desk paraphernalia in pull-out scoops borrowed from the kitchen. Another unique touch is the old mailbox set into the straw-matted wall.

Trimly tailored for a family that retreats here for music, television and books, this is a den that goes a long way to eliminate guest-work. Sofa simply opens for sleeping and shades pull down for privacy. A family project, the room has homemade shelf unit, corduroy-covered walls and screens, coordinated with braid trim.

BATHROOM IDEAS

The Romans had the right idea about bathrooms. They turned them into elegant, attractive places to be, filled with all the luxuries that made life nicer two millennia or so ago. For a while there, we turned our backs on the Romans' ideas, and turned baths into sterile, all-white rooms, with no room for imagination. Then came today's bathroom renaissance, and a new kind of luxury even the emperors would envy. There are high-fashion coverings for floors and walls, fancy faucet sets, towels, shower curtains and such, designed by world-famous stylists. Put them together and they'll bring even a drab bathroom with no natural endowments a long way toward attractiveness. So will a fillip or two of originality. Even with all the exciting new offerings designed just for the bath, you can still bring in bright new ideas from other sources. There's one important prerequisite to all the decorating fun—good lighting. It, too, comes nicely packaged these days, and it's almost impossible to buy too much, since the bath should be about the brightest room in the house. Most of the baths coming up on the next nine pages had a lot going for them in the beginning. But still they are filled with ideas worth scaling down for even the mini-est of rooms. You'll see that small spaces needn't limit you to small ideas . . . that "foreign" furniture originally intended for other rooms can add new personality to a bath . . . and so can a bit of whimsy.

Skylight windows in a bath—what a lovely problem to cope with! Roller shades are the practical solution for light and privacy control on a string. Braid trim keeps them from looking too practical, however. In fact, this enormous bath looks anything but plain practical with its rich colors and unusual ingredients like the leather chair, glass table and patterned rug.

More bottoms-up shades maintain privacy in the unusually well-windowed bathroom above. Designed by Edward Durell Stone, the house looks out on lots of Long Island, N.Y., woods. So it's unnecessary to keep the windows always covered. Up-and-down shades solve the problem—and add decorative punch with bright bands of carpet braid that pick up the wallpaper colors. Don't miss the revitalized scale.

Wicker arches give architectural interest to an erstwhile ordinary bath, right. The usual sink-toilet lineup against the wall opposite the tub is broken by one arch angling over the lavatory. The second becomes a vanity niche, backed by mirrors and lighted by a tole lamp. Glass shelves and bright floral paper keep the limited space looking uncluttered. Real flowers (they thrive on moisture) are another fresh touch.

This handsome bath would rate applause from a Roman emperor, but its elegance is mainly a matter of imagination. Easy-to-build wooden shelves and valances take away the bathroom look. Panels of fabric to match the draperies are edged in yellow slats covered with trim. The metal étagère, with its classic accessories, is the final touch.

179

Most powder rooms go pretty and provincial with flowery paper and crystal light fixtures. We go in the opposite direction for an almost op art effect in an extra bath, left. Less complicated than it looks, the canopy and base around the lavatory are made of poplin plywood bent to shape and painted, like the walls, in super swirls.

Shade, shower curtain and accessories in the bathroom above are all made from vinyl that already looks wet. Such coordination begins with the home fashions industry, which is putting more and more emphasis on products for attractive bathrooms. Not strictly for the bath but also attractive on the job are a wicker stand and ottoman.

The unexpected adds interest to all three bathrooms on these pages. Above, the pleasant surprise is the Early American theme, authentic
right down to the braided rug and antique washstand
with its marble top. Wall rack, now used for guest
towels, and cane-bottomed chair are also antiques.
New but nice are plank walls and print paper.

There's room for the whole family in the smallish townhouse bathroom above. The portrait gallery that stretches wall-to-wall is a nice bit of whimsy, especially since the vintage pictures complement the up-dated gas lamps that light the mirror. Another novel touch is the giant towel-turned-shower-curtain. A radiator lurks behind the doors of the "cabinet."

Instead of scuttling the grand old footed bathtub when they went to remodeling their up-state New York house, right, the young couple kept both it and their sense of humor. With double rows of fringe glued under the lip, and handsome towel curtains, the tub is now the grand dame of the bathroom. Both walls and carpeting are moisture-resistant.

APARTMENT LIVING

Despite the great American exodus from cities to suburbs, more and more of us have become apartment-dwellers. At some point for nearly everyone, an apartment offers the best way of life. Young careerists flock into them, living happily on shoestrings and serendipities from the Salvation Army. Young marrieds bring the same imagination and a bit more money to their apartments, where they usually stay until the first offspring arrives. Then, as soon as the children are grown and gone, it's back to the convenience of an apartment. With someone else tending the furnace, grass and other tasks, there's more time for living, a principle that's fostered the development of apartments at vacation resorts and retirement villages. There's another side to the coin, of course. Apartments are infamous for their lack of space, cramped closets, miniature kitchens. Their rooms are erratic in size and shape—or else boringly alike—and they're filled with inherent headaches like awkward beams and unlovable pipes. Decorating an apartment is a special art. In most cases, it calls for scaling down furniture size and playing up coordination between the rooms, double-duty furnishings, everything to give more livability in limited space. The possibilities are much less limited than that space. Let's look at some ideas to give your apartment a new lease on life, and more living room for anyone with space problems.

Color both divides and unifies typical living-dining room on opposite page. Bright red on the sofa, which is set at a right angle to break up the open floor plan, is echoed against the opposite wall by dramatic, ceiling-high screens. Covered to match the sofa and trimmed with the same braid, the screens are homemade of pine shelving and free-standing for easy mobility.

One look at this handsome apartment and suddenly you understand why we praise things for being "done up brown." The skylight windows and a generous helping of white keep the brown from going too dark. At once sophisticated and yet comfortable, the room is well-arranged for both work and entertaining. Every seating unit has ample lamp-light.

*S*ophisticated spot for dining has been claimed in one corner of this New York City high-rise, left. Since it overlooks the terrace and is surrounded by glass, dressing the windows and door could have posed problems. Shades are the simple solution, accented with tassels and banners of braid to conceal the separations between them, and the rollers across the top. Potted plants contribute a garden atmosphere.

*S*hades again, this time the roman variety used unobtrusively over skylight windows in another Manhattan apartment, above. Short windows below are covered with cafes in a solid gold fabric which picks up the stripes featured on the sofa, table and upholstered dining stools. The other furnishings are an interestingly eclectic mixture, all collected in Europe by the fashion designer who lives here.

Color is a sure way to achieve a kind of continuity throughout an apartment. As long as you have that color bridge between rooms, you can vary patterns and accents from place to place without producing a hodge-podge. The living room above follows naturally on the entry below, where the bright red is first met.

In addition to the point about color carry-over, the hallway shows what every apartment–dweller knows—that every square foot should be put to use. Left, a dining area that seats six has been slipped in against what would have been a non-working wall. In order to achieve the private atmosphere conducive to gracious dining, the front door has been curtained from view.

The euphemistically named "efficiency" apartment—one room with many lives to lead. There's seldom space enough to divide physically, but psychologically there are many ways to accomplish the job. Two good ones are at work, opposite. The sofa is set at an angle and backed by a divider of braid and brass rods.

Black-and-white, plus one super-color, sparkle in both these apartment rooms. Besides the color schemes, there are other ideas worth borrowing. Boy's bedroom below suffered two standard apartment bugaboos: radiator under the window and structural beams over it. Tall, thin shutters take care of the first problem. They fold flat over the striped shades, and the few inches of space lost behind them is more than recouped by the shelves built under—and disguising—the beam.

Divide by adding a colorful, free-swinging partition. Made of fluffy Pom Decors, cotton pompons strung on fiber glass strands and hung from a special rod, the divider separates one big apartment room into two areas for living and dining without actually closing off the space. The stripes carry on the snappy black-white-and-green color scheme that runs between the "rooms." The area rug in the living side and angled arrangement of the dining furniture further clarify the division.

So many modern apartments seem to have come from the same page in some architect's guidebook. Here's that ubiquitous row of windows again, with the radiator underneath. They've been dealt with in note-worthy fashion, however. Short cafe curtains cover the radiator; shades control the daylight; full draperies draw at night.

There's more than one way to win the space race in an open-plan apartment room. Modern way of thinking, above, leads to division by leather-covered panels, which are repeated across the window in the rear. Bright yellow and bordered with braid, the dividers complement the color scheme that carries over to the dining area.

The more traditional-minded can have their space and divide it, too, simply by relying on the angled-sofa arrangement. Flanked by a lamp table and backed by the drop leaf dining table, the sofa breaks up space without sacrificing any. One large, fringed rug runs right under to unify the areas, and windows are treated alike.

ound: *the missing dining room! Found by imaginative apartment dwellers who had to turn to their own devices in lieu of preplanned floor space. All three dining rooms on these pages have been eked out of other areas. Above, a one-room studio apartment becomes two, visually, with the addition of a simple wood frame divider woven with braid. Rugs also set off the dining group.*

Denizens of a big city high-rise decided that one could dine formally, even in a foyer, if the space were handled dramatically. It is, above, where walls are laced with large print paper. The door (to the kitchen) is set off with bright, painted squares and wild, flowered draperies, tied high to permit easy passage. Furnishings look light in glass and cane.

Creating a room out of thin air, literally, divider is made from lumber panels covered to match the draperies across the dining area wall in the rear. The painting hangs on narrow wood strips which have been faced with more of the braid that conceals fabric edges on the panels. Painting is backed with another painting facing the dining area.

IV THE WIDE WIDE WORLD OF WINDOWS

Windows mean communication–between the outside world and the inside, and within the home itself. Decoratively speaking, they tell the room's story, whether it's elegantly phrased in silks and velvet, or couched in casual terms of burlap cafe curtains. Windows are the most important decorating subject of all because they tell a two-fold tale–of fashion and of function. They are there to let in the air, light and the view, too, if it's nice. And they can be dressed in many fashions without interfering with those basic functions. As you're about to see in this idea-filled section, there are dozens of attractive–and practical–ways to approach the subject of wide, wide windows.

*F*ormal elegance for a formal room opposite, but not without a problem first—and from the very arch that makes this such a lovely window. The solution lay in the solid color swags, shaped to follow the window frame and tacked precisely in place. A border of trimming around the arch conceals the mechanics and outlines the treatment. Side jabots are lined with the same print fabric used for the gathered austrian shade and to cover the walls and window seat cushion. In the world of window dressing, this is truly haute couture.

ormer windows, with their special indentations, offer ready-made opportunities for overall treatments. An extroverted flower print carries the show for both dormers on this page. Left, the entire window area was fabricked inside, even the frame. Then a plywood valance was trimmed to match the shade.

lowered fabric and matching wallpaper frolic over window, wall and ceiling, then down across the beds and their upholstered heads in the dormer room at the right. The shirred curtains are tied back over a shade which has been appliquéd with flowers cut from the fabric. The rug, table and window sill accessories play up the print.

Novel window for a little big game hunter, above, is made with plywood and rug fringe "thatching." Fringe is stapled to the frame, which is anchored to the window top—"spear" curtain rods are mainly for show. So are the strap curtains, hung at window-sill height over blank wall. Matching rod and strap arrangement holds a covered pillow, which serves as a headboard for the bed. Under the thatched roof, a roller shade, in burlap to match wallcovering, controls light.

Eight tablespoons of imagination go into the kitchen window concoction at left. Sections of cotton gingham are cut separately, then sewn together with slots on the back to hold the wooden spoons. Just for fun, the window shade is laminated with cookbook pages. Windows like these are just for fun, for places like kitchens and children's rooms, where they are charming in small doses.

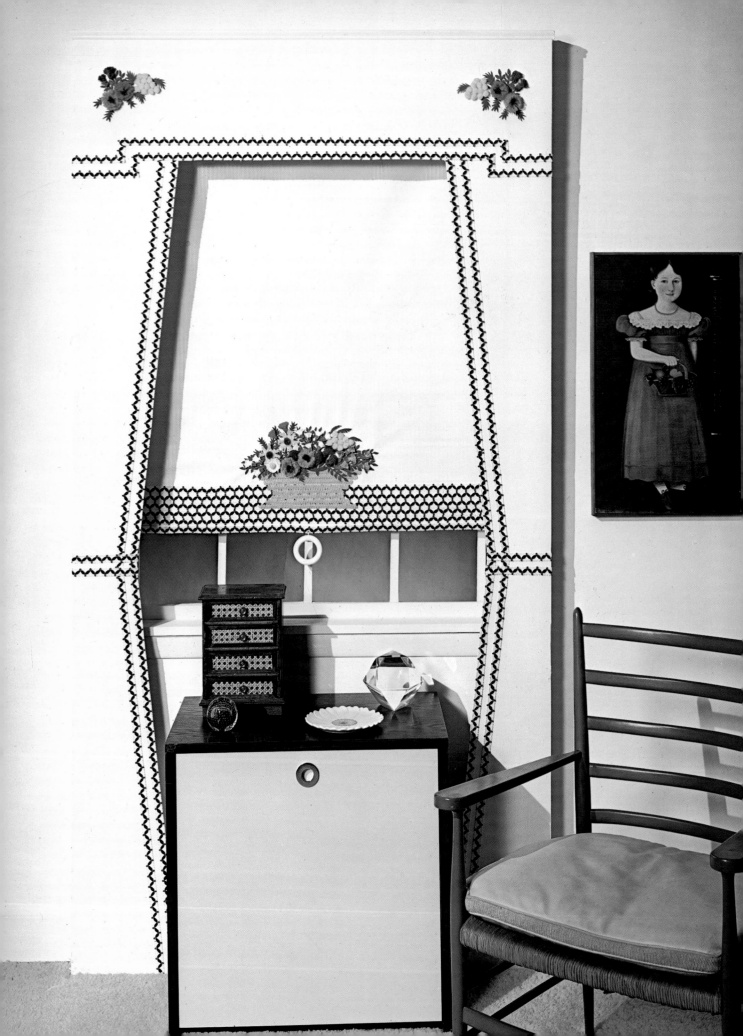

Trompe l'oeil with tongue in cheek, the tie-back "curtains" on the preceding page are actually made with a hammer and saw. A painted plywood lambrequin is shaped like curtains and trimmed with braid to carry forth the illusion. Beneath the lambrequin is a plain shade that has burst into bloom. The basketful of flowers is made with bits and pieces of various fringes and felt, cut and glued to form flowers and leaves. The dimensional floral motif is repeated on the upper corners of the lambrequin.

Another kind of window frame-up enlists the aid of braid to create an optical illusion. Above, a wooden frame has been set, wall-to-wall, over a smallish window and its rectangular openings edged with red paint. Behind each opening is stapled a lattice of white braid, woven so its edges form the quatrefoil design. Then blue felt is used to back the braid and create the tri-color scheme that picks up the room's reds-whites-and-blues. Overall, the frame adds drama and dimension to a ho-hum window.

Merry spiral for a youthful bedroom window features triple rows of ball fringe, which pick up the colors in the wallpaper and matching fabric, and—equally important—are the secret of the unusual jabot's success. The weight of the fringe keeps the spirals hanging in place once they are coiled down the sides of the window. Made all in one piece of fabric, twice as long as the three sides it will cover, the strip is smocked across the top and gathered down sides (using ready-made shirr tape).

Simple fabric panels and laminated shade turn a small, square window into a contemporary coup. The window is really only inches wider than what you see, but it feels hugely important in the room since the eye-filling side panels seem to stretch it out across the wall. Hung on a single brass rod, they are weighted with matching rods at the bottom. The shade is made with a laminating kit, of fabric in a geometric print that plays off nicely against the panels. Note its matching cuff and braid trim.

More than a mere shade of difference results in each of these three rooms when shades are used to dress the windows. They don't stop there, in the room above. The lower shelves of the bookcases are also covered by roller shades, installed bottoms-up behind wood frames to keep them in place. Trimming matches window shades.

Store-bought striped shade, left, is sprinkled with stenciled-on stars. Black ball fringe and tassel pull repeat the mood of the black-striped vinyl floor. A special fun touch for this whimsical window is the flower box suspended on chains below the shutters.

Uproarious rainbow brightens the life of the baby who lives in the nursery on the opposite page. The bouncy print is laminated onto the window shade, made into pert little gathered cafes and cushion, then used to wrap the homemade étagère. Fringe echoes the colors on the shelves, which are great for showing and stowing toys.

Two ordinary windows become one handsome architectural unit, above, when they are united behind a lambrequin. It and the roller shades are both faced with vinyl fabric that emulates wood, then given bright stripes of self-sticking ribbon to tie them in with the fabric on walls and cafe curtains. Small braid dressmaker frogs pair off across the ribbon to give a dimensional effect.

Old Glory colors brighten the boy's window, opposite, and pick up the mood of the wallcovering. A trimly tailored roman shade, the banner is made by sewing together three equal widths of fabric. Tri-color tassels and the window frame outlined in red complete the cheerful treatment. Roman shades adapt well for any window where curtains or draperies might be too fussy.

I mportant as they are, windows can't do their best decorating work alone. They should play back to the rest of the room, repeating a fabric, color or at least a feeling from somewhere else. The smallish window here gets its *Wow!* by reflecting the rich fabric that covers the bed, its head and the homemade nightstands. Also for emphasis: the shaped braid outline glued around the window.

Breakfast in bed, almost. It's a treat anytime, but made especially attractive when it's served in style, opposite. Frame for the table is a simple, square lambrequin, covered with shirred strips to match the bedspread fabric. Inside the frame, gathered curtains are trimmed and tied back with a narrow version of the braid that crisscrosses the table. The bright pink accent color is nicely cross-referenced all around the bedroom.

A bit of fashion history repeats itself atop the tall, thin window, above. This elaborate old brass cornice was loved during Victorian times but lost until the owner of the Manhattan townhouse brought it back as the perfect complement to the period pieces in the small study. Draperies, with their swag and jabot, are also appropriate, though their colors are zestily modern. The braid trim reappears on chair, blinds and the ceramic stool.

Roll out the carpet...right on up around the window for this well-coordinated bedroom. The trellis design of the rug adapts naturally to the shaped lambrequin that embraces the window (it was carefully planned to keep the carpet's design intact). The remnant from the center of the lambrequin covers a curve of Upson board to make a matching bolster for the bed. Colors in the spread, campaign chests and sheer curtains inside the lambrequin echo the carpet.

Bouffant curtains, above, are just the right, frothy thing for this very feminine bedroom window to wear. Sewing is simpler than it looks, since side panels are single strips with a rod channel stitched in at each pouf section. Valance is made separately, with the same bubbly bottom, and gathered onto a rod over the side panels. Use very full, sheer fabric for the right effect.

On the other hand, you can have this perky little window treatment without sewing a stitch. It's made from Pom Decors, fluffy cotton "beads" strung on fiber glass cords. Special rods accommodate the top pompon, which simply slips into a channel, and the curtain is made. The colors, left, are chosen to repeat the cheerful print of the washable kitchen wall covering.

Plain venetian blind is dressed to prove the point that a little fabric can go a long way toward decorating a room. Flowers cut from scraps of the print that makes the quilted bed cover, opposite, have been glued, strip by strip, onto the slats of the venetian blind. (It's a simple matter of ruling the flowers to measure before cutting.) Fringed curtain hems match the colors.

F avored for French doors, draperies tied back in the center can do
special things for a series of windows, too. Above, the trim treatment marches around an Early Americanish bedroom, made in
fabric to match the bed canopy and cover, and the upholstered chair.
Sheer curtains are stretched beneath the tie-backs, which are trimmed
with ball fringe to soften their precise, hourglass outline. One of the
most versatile of drapery styles, tie-backs can be caught high or low,
and held by all manner of objects for various effects.

L ouvered lambrequin is a great frame-up for the very tailored window on the opposite page. And it's simple to build since the three
panels can be bought ready-made and painted. Here, the sides are
set on wood bases for added height. Decorative braid and giant drawer
pulls, which have been covered with the drapery fabric, punctuate the
panels. Matching braid outlines the draw draperies hung on a rod
mounted inside the lambrequin itself.

Bouncy and bright, in red, orange and white, this is a window idea worth repeating—so it is, in the scalloped bed throw with its braid and big pompon tiebacks. Even the bed head shapes up to match. It's homemade of wood, slightly padded and wrapped in the same fabric as the bed's dust ruffles and round bolster. The wood rods and rings at the window are painted tangy red like the end wall, and hung so they show off against the white frame.

Tie-backs take naturally to trimming, and not necessarily the same kind in both directions. Here are two new slants on the tie-back theme. Above, braid and tassels combine to outline both the elegantly full draperies and the simple valance. The holdbacks are worth noting, too. They are sculptured brass medallions set at window-sill height so the fabric gathers and falls in a graceful diagonal down the wall. The whole window is done in soft green and gold which play back to the carpet and walls.

Opposite, a repeat performance from the floor to the wall . . . with one interesting difference. The same thick wool knot fringe that borders the area rug runs down the smocked draperies and serves as tie-backs. But the fringe is variegated green-and-blue on the floor. At the window, the colors go their separate ways for a subtle touch of whimsy. Accessories are carefully selected to pick up the blue-and-green interaction. The rug is a rectangle, scissored into its interesting shape before fringing.

Tie-back draperies needn't be simply tied-back with the customary circles of matching fabric. There are many ways to do the job and gain added interest for the whole window treatment. This quintet of ideas includes chains, left, used as rings over the painted rod and linked in various lengths.

Simple additions turn the usual fabric bands into unusual accents for a window. An ascot effect is achieved, top, by tacking two shaped and trimmed sections to the tie-back. Below, a lined quarter-circle of fabric is layered in fringe before being stitched to the band.

A blow well-struck in decorating deserves a black belt as much as any karate champion. And it wins the honors, above, with a belt made from black vinyl, studded with eyelets and caught with a buckle from the notions counter. Handsome in a black-and-white room.

Twice-over brightly with black-and-white scallops gives double the impact to the simple draperies at the right. Both the valance and tie-backs are backed with Permette buckram and edged with black ball fringe. Permette can be shaped conveniently with scissors, sewn on a machine and hung on an ordinary rod.

Wall-to-wall windows are dressed in elegant roman shades under a double valance. As sensible as they are sumptuous for this Long Island, N.Y., living room, the shades require less fabric than draperies, open completely to show off the view, and don't interfere with the French doors, left under lowered shade. Tasseled velvet strips to match under-valances conceal corner separations.

Two rooms, too close to go their separate ways, decoratively, yet with different window problems. In the dining room, left, the windows were smallish and unimportant, while they filled almost the entire living room wall, above. Since the two rooms adjoin, the same colors are used as common denominators throughout, although the prints at the windows are different. So is the clever way of adding emphasis with fabric-filled wood frames.

Three little windows that could have jumbled up the whole living room wall, above, are smoothed into one dramatic treatment behind a long valance and sheer undercurtains. The fabric of the flanking draperies is repeated on the sofa, and the fringe reappears on the table cloth and in the dining room. More repetition-with-a-purpose: dining room fabric on living room chair, and vice versa. The same carpet runs wall-to-wall in both rooms.

Here is one way to make the utmost of the big picture windows that are so much a part of the American scene, both in the suburbs and city apartments. An overall, covered wood valance, left, plays up the window without interfering with its practical purpose. Underneath the trimmed and tasseled valance, a triple play of roman shades gives easy access to the movable side windows (behind the tie-back draperies).

A bay becomes a lively and livable corner with the clever arrangement of draperies, above, that goes to all lengths to dramatize the window. Center panels (which will open for added light) go midway down, meeting the side panels to frame the lacquered Parsons table. Maxi-length side draperies will swing free from their tie-backs for complete coverage at night, showing the bold geometric fabric off to full advantage.

V SERENDIPITIES

Truly original rooms always contain a serendipity or two, that extra–and often unexpected–touch that's such a delight to discover. Serendipities can pull things together, decoratively speaking. They can add accent or accomplish a practical purpose. And, since they're often homegrown ideas, they almost always make people wonder, "Why didn't *I* think of that?" There's a sense of humor about most serendipities, but never a sense of contrivance. Gadgetry doesn't count. Nor do devices that serve only to amuse. Eleven pages of serendipities are coming up to show what we mean. In every case, they're only a small part of an overall plan, but the small part they play makes a big difference in the total effectiveness of the room.

Screen steals the scene in the sunny south-of-the-border dining room on the opposite page. Even if it had been left bland, a screen would have been a good idea, because its floor-to-ceiling height hides the unlovely heating duct that spoiled the room's corner. But a mile of imagination, plus a few yards of fabric and fringes, turns a good idea into a serendipity. The fabric is cut on the diagonal and wrapped around plain pine shelving, then the fringes are added along the stripes for three-dimensional drama.

*L*ittle things can make the big difference between a room
that's attractive and one that is really interesting,
that looks as if the furnishings were planned, not
merely assembled. The little thing that brings this bedroom into focus is woven braid, used in three different
widths. Four inches wide, it runs around the room's ceiling line and down over the loose pillows and velvet bedspread. A narrower version trims the fabric-covered
screens at the windows and the matching, smocked bed
curtains. Then, finally, the thinnest (less than an inch
wide) is used to point up the quartet of pictures over the
bed. Without the added attraction of the braids, the bedroom would still be soft and serenely pretty, above. But
the trimmings make it a room to be remembered.

When baby makes three and there's only one bedroom in the apartment, think serendipity. A large closet can convert to a cozy nursery, above, without upsetting the whole household. Shelves and doors removed, the inside of the closet is brightened with paint and a ready-made strip of lights attached to the ceiling, unseen behind the canopy. Draperies, kept tied back during the day, slide closed at night for everyone's privacy. Unlikely looking but very handy, the Parsons table-desk doubles as a diapering area. Powders, puffs, etceteras are concealed in the wicker basket on top.

The guest who comes to dinner can linger on for breakfast if you hide him away in the cupboard. Not so uncomfortable as it sounds, when the dining room includes a serendipity, as does the one above. A hidden bed folds down from the sleek, cane-fronted cupboard, ready for overnight duty. Shelves in the adjoining cabinet can be cleared for the guest's convenience. And without even rearranging the furniture, there's room for one more. Such double-duty furniture is a special boon to apartment dwellers and represents a bit of one-upmanship over the more ordinary sleep-sofa.

Beauty is truly in the eye of the beholder. The ingredients of the whimsical art wall, above, don't look like much in their natural state. But seen through the eyes of a serendipity-seeker, they come on like works of art. Included are salt spoons and cookie cutters; pasta; brass light switch plates; coasters, spoons and corks; tasseled fly swatters; tin mold; chopsticks and braid; grater; wire whisk "balloon;" party favor still life.

Art underfoot is a fun do-it-yourself project that can be completed in an evening or so. The colorful rug is created from Pom Decors, fluffy cotton pompons that come strung on fiber glass cords. The Pom Decors are cut into strips or individual pompons and either glued or sewn to a muslin backing. The design for the "floor painting" on the opposite page was borrowed from wallpaper simply by placing the muslin over the paper and tracing.

Doors often suffer from an open-and-shut case of neglect. We walk through most of them without really seeing them. Not the handsome door on the opposite page, at least not since its once-plain face has been lifted with half-round wooden molding glued on within a frame of 1″x3″ pine strips. Stained, the door stars in the Mediterranean room.

Christmas comes but once a year, but gift-giving and wrapping go on around the calendar, usually with a long search beforehand for paper, ribbon, scissors, etc. Obviate the problem with a gift chest, which holds within its drawers everything you need, including small, miscellaneous gifts. The chest above was a Salvation Army find, right. Revived with paint and inscribed with cut-outs from wrapping paper and dimestore letters, it's now the first stop for all happy occasions.

The coming of central heating and the going of superstitions about "night vapours" have cast the bed canopy in an entirely decorative role. Once, it had to be elaborate and multi-layered to protect the bed's occupants. Now it can be simply elegant, like the one at the left. Braid-trimmed velveteen on bed and bolster merely runs up the wall and over a painted board attached there with angle irons.

Space, found in surprising ways, can be the best serendipity of all. This wall was almost unemployed because the young couple's furniture budget ran dry. Ingenuity to the rescue: plain wooden shelves are suspended—on cup hooks—from chains anchored to ceiling and through rug to the floor. Edged in the orange of the wallpaper, shelves now hold books, plants, baskets for jewelry, etc.

VI

HOME FURNISHINGS LEXICON

HOW TO BUY THE BEST FOR YOUR HOME

T ime was when things were made of silk or cotton, wood, wool or metal. There just wasn't much more to choose from, and so, in a way, the choosing was easier. Today, we live in a man-made world of multi-media. There's an almost bewildering array of materials on the home furnishings market, with more rolling out of industry's test tubes every minute —marvelous materials that won't rumple, wrinkle or fade; fabrics that look like leather and wear like iron; plastics that look like wood and work like magic to resist heat, scratches, stains. Today, we can dress our windows in "silk" no worm ever saw, cover our floors in "marble" that never came from a quarry, panel our walls in "walnut" no tree had to lay down its life for.

It's an exciting place, this man-made world, and things are so much easier to take care of than in the "good old days."

But all this choice can make it harder to choose, unless you understand and appreciate the characteristics of the various new materials. It takes a well-informed shopper to know what she's getting for her home furnishings money today. And that's what this section is all about, to help translate the labels on your purchases, to help you know which of the new materials best meets your needs...or if you want to rely on one of Nature's old favorites. For modern technology hasn't passed them by in its rush to innovation. Wool has a new look, cotton a new wearability, wood new finishes that let it go on living quite comfortably in modern interiors.

All this is not to say that everything under the sun is new. Furniture styles go on and on...Queen Anne is every bit as elegant today as it was nearly three centuries ago, and the Colonial Williamsburg look is as popular as ever. So an understanding of historic furniture styles is prerequisite for any decorating venture. So is an understanding of how to buy quality in furniture, and how to arrange it for the best looks and livability. You must also understand how drapery hardware works, how floor coverings differ, how to select the right paint and paper for your walls. The following pages will show you how, so that the dollars you spend will buy attractive furnishings you'll like living with for a long, long time.

THE RIGHT ROOM ARRANGEMENT

A good room arrangement ranks right up there with color as the least expensive, most important element in interior design. The most elegant furniture assemblage in the world won't add up to an attractive room if it is impractically arranged. But put a room together well and you will enjoy looking at it and living in it, no matter what the ingredients. In short a good furniture arrangement *functions*, it is *comfortable*, and pleases the eye like a well-composed painting.

On top of all that, it's not difficult to achieve. There are definite guidelines you can follow with success almost assured. Before you even begin to move a room around mentally, arm yourself with graph paper from the stationery store. Now use a metal rule—repeat, *metal* rule because it won't stretch—to measure your room, including dimensions of fireplace, windows, doors and any other architectural elements. Outline the room on the graph paper, making 1/4 inch equal one foot. Indicate which way doors open; windows, too, if necessary. Measure the furniture you intend to use and sketch each piece to the same scale on the graph paper. Label, color to match the actual places and cut them out.

Now, with your problem miniaturized before you, you're ready for the guidelines that will help solve it. The big *first:* consider the room's function, or functions, as it's more likely to be in this multi-purpose age. For example, in one home a living room may be exactly that, the major "public" area in which the whole family entertains, watches television, relaxes or enjoys meals, if one end is set aside for dining. In another home, the living room may be a formal area, mainly reserved for guests, while a family room elsewhere takes over most of the activities. Obviously, the arrangements in these two living rooms would be quite different, each based on the purpose it serves.

Rethink your own family's living habits. Consider what will go on in each room. Then select the furniture that will meet those needs.

Now have another look at your scale drawing of the room. Decide how traffic will flow through it, from one door to another, from door to closet, etc., and lightly pencil arrows in each direction. You can "bend" those arrows somewhat as your arrangement dictates, but don't try to reroute traffic too drastically from its natural paths.

That takes care of the most important practical considerations. On to the esthetics: Build your room around at least one focal point. A fireplace is classic. Lacking one, you may choose a window with a good view. Or, if you have no outstanding architectural centerpiece, you may play up a handsome painting, an unusual rug, an important piece of furniture. Start your grouping by settling the largest piece of furniture first, then work the others around it. Remember as you go • That seating pieces should be close enough for quiet conversation • That every chair needs a nearby table to hold its occupant's drink, ashtray and such • That every chair should be well lighted, both by day and night • That tables should be used only when there's a functional need for them • That several occasional chairs should be stationed around the room to be drawn into the main grouping as the occasion requires. Area rugs can be used quite successfully to underscore a grouping, to set off various activity centers in a large room. So can lighting, from both pendant fixtures and more dramatic recessed spots that illuminate different areas.

Try to avoid catercornering furniture—it never looks as if you meant it. Place sofas, tables, etc., at right angles to the wall only when there's plenty of room left for movement around them; plan at least two-foot-wide traffic lanes, three-foot clearance at doorways. And try to keep things balanced around the room from several points of view: (1) Number of pieces. Don't crowd too much into one grouping. Counterbalance with secondary arrangements in the opposite end of the room or along the opposite wall. (2) Within each grouping. For example, two chairs with a table between "weigh" as much as a sofa. (3) Vertically. Each room requires some tall pieces as counterpoint for the horizontal lines of sofa, tables, etc., which usually predominate. Use étagères, grandfather clocks, even a tall arrangement of artworks on the wall. (4) Color- and pattern-wise. Remember that dark colors and bright patterns draw the eye away from light hues and solids so they look heavier in a room. Don't cluster like pieces;

Usually, it's the open-plan rooms—living, family rooms, etc.—that offer the most flexibility, and, therefore, the most puzzlement when it comes to furniture arranging. Bedrooms, even when they're big enough to offer several alternatives, usually come with only one wall wide enough for the bed. As a general rule, twin beds in a master bedroom are placed parallel; elsewhere, they may be arranged against the walls to free more floor space.

With all the guidelines in mind, start arranging your little paper furniture around your scale model room. When you have a plan that pleases you, trace the furniture pieces onto the floor plan. Now follow it to create the real thing!

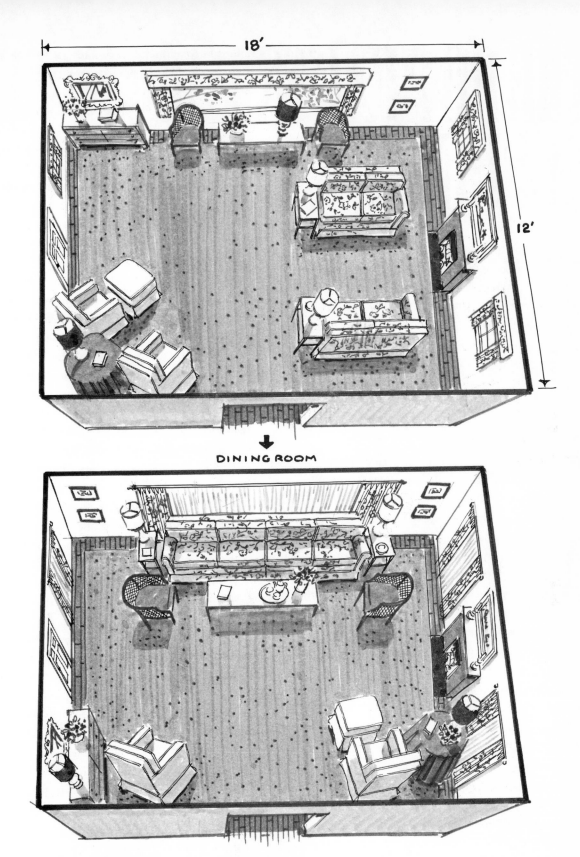

18'

12'

DINING ROOM

FURNITURE ARRANGEMENT CAN CONTROL the looks, livability and overall impact of any room. Although the layout, top, is well balanced, it's too disjointed to be congenial, with its seating arrangements scattered to three areas. A bit of shifting produces a more workable room, bottom. The focal point is switched from the fireplace to the large window, where sofas are butted and flanked by cane chairs. Easy chairs now contribute to the group and the formerly forgotten coffee table becomes a convenience center.

CARPET FACTS AND FIBERS

As the underlying star of the home fashions show, carpeting has held the floor, literally, since at least 3000 B.C. The Egyptians get the credit for creating the first woven rugs recorded by history, but surely before that cavemen used animal skin "scatter rugs." In general, multi-color, or tweed surfaces tend to take soil more in stride than solid colors, especially very light or dark solids. But don't think you have to rush back to the beige wave that flooded America's floors a few decades ago. Your carpet dealer has a whole paintbox of colors, colors as practical as they are pretty.

We've come full-cycle—fur rugs are back with us. But other things have changed amazingly underfoot since the Pharaohs' time. Modern technology has made carpeting, once the right of royalty only, a fact of everyday life for every homemaker. It's also made possible wall-to-wall carpeting, broadloom rugs much wider than any ancient weaver's loom, rugs treated to eliminate static electricity, and floor coverings that shrug off spills, stains, insects, mildew, dry rot, sun and rain, both inside the house and out onto the terrace and patio. New, too, on the modern scene are carpet tiles, self-adhering squares you can install yourself, and carpets designed for walls, not floors.

Today, your choice is almost unlimited, in terms of colors, of materials, of sizes, surface finishes—and in terms of costs. The best rule to follow in the latter case is the old one: buy the best you can afford. Poor quality carpeting is never a bargain, although there are some low traffic areas where you can

afford to compromise. Bedrooms get less wear, for example. But you should be prepared to spend the money you save there on high quality carpeting for the stairs, hallway, living room, if it's a busy place. Often, rug makers offer look-alike products in a range of qualities and prices, so you can vary your cost according to use without sacrificing coordination. Use will also help determine the surface texture of the carpeting you choose. Among the surface treatments available are: (1) **PLUSH,** with thick, deep-cut pile; (2) **LOOP,** where the pile yarns are left uncut. Loop surfaces may be all one height, multi-level for a patterned effect as shown, or combined with cut yarns (3); (4) **TWIST,** where the surface yarns are corkscrewed to give a pebbly effect. A **SCULPTURED** or **CARVED** surface is sheared at different levels to produce a design. **SHEARED,** or **TIP-SHEARED,** means the surface pile has been cut to produce a plush surface. **SHAGS** feature long, loose surface yarns, while **FLAT WEAVES,** with almost no surface textures, have been rediscovered of late.

In general, plush surfaces are favored for formal interiors and for less trafficked areas since they tend to show foot prints. Dense loop, loop-and-plush combinations and twist surfaces tend to stand up well underfoot; use them for stairs and hallways. Shags are especially super in modern settings where their soft richness provides the perfect foil for hard-edge steel and glass furniture. For period rooms, you can find elegant orientals, both the real thing and less expensive domestic versions. For Early American or provincial interiors, hook, braided and rag rugs abound.

When it comes to the size of your floor coverings, there are four basic choices: area rugs, room-size rugs, room-fit rugs and wall-to-wall carpeting.

AREA RUGS come in all sizes and shapes, and are generally used to set off an area of the room from the rest of the flooring. **ROOM-SIZE RUGS** come close (within 8 to 12 inches) to the walls, leaving a definite border of floor showing on all sides. **ROOM-FIT RUGS** touch the walls and look like wall-to-wall carpeting, except that they can be taken up easily for cleaning. Installed **WALL-TO-WALL CARPETING,** which seems to have become a kind of status symbol, is a fairly permanent thing, and installation ups the price proportionately. You *can* have it taken up and reinstalled when you move, but it must be cleaned on the floor and cannot be turned to distribute wear and tear. However, it can add an impressive air of spaciousness when it flows from one room to another.

There are other factors to know before you buy floor coverings. First, understand the kinds of fibers you'll find in rugs today, both on the surface and underneath. Law requires manufacturers to identify the carpet contents on the label, and, while each manufacturer may have his own trade name for the synthetics, the fiber will fall under one of these classifications:

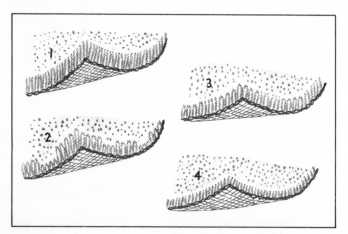

ACRYLIC (and Modacrylic)

Man-made fibers that look and feel very much like wool. Resilient, highly soil- and stain-resistant, easy to clean, durable.

BI-CONSTITUENT FIBER

New blend of nylon and polyester. Resilient, durable, silky.

COTTON

Nature's budget fiber. Soils and crushes easily, but washes readily and wears well.

NYLON

Strongest man-made fiber. Long-wearing, easy to care for, highly moisture-resistant. Nylon will be found as "continuous filaments" (long strands used in loop pile carpets) and as "staple" nylon (short strands spun into yarn). Avoid cheap products which tend to fuzz.

POLYESTER

Man-made fiber with wool-like luxury, nylon-like strength. Also found as staple or continuous filaments. Durable, resilient, resists soil and water-borne stains, chemicals, abrasion and sunlight. Easy to clean.

POLYPROPYLENE (olefin)

Extremely strong, lightweight man-made fiber. Very resistant to stains, moisture, fading. Makes outdoor carpeting practical.

WOOL

Time-honored carpet favorite by which other fibers are measured. Excellent resiliency, soil resistance, durability. Most wool carpets are now permanently mothproofed — check the label. A new "super crimped" wool has now been developed.

RAYON

Usually found in area rugs. Tends to be less resilient than other fibers but gives good service in low-traffic areas.

BACKING

The backing itself is another important point to consider. Usually made of jute, polypropylene or olefin fiber, it will then be covered with latex to bind the yarns. Good quality tufted carpets will have an additional layer on top of this known as "double backing."

CONSTRUCTION

The carpet you buy today will probably be constructed by one of three methods: tufting, weaving or knitting.

WEAVING

The traditional method; you will find woven carpets referred to as *Axminster*, *velvet* or *Wilton*. These are the types of looms used, not an indication of quality.

TUFTING

A newer, faster, less costly means of construction now accounts for the great majority of carpets. A many-needled machine inserts pile tufts into a prewoven backing.

KNITTING

A less frequently employed process, loops surface and backing yarns together by machine.

NEEDLE PUNCHING

A new technique by which fibers are punched into a structural material, then compressed into a felt-like fabric. Used mainly for indoor-outdoor carpets.

FLOCKING

Another new means of construction in which short pile fibers are electrostatically adhered to a foundation layer to produce a cut pile surface with a velvety look.

You will also find **PRINTED** carpets, where, as the name implies, designs are printed on the finished carpet's surface.

Whatever method of construction is used, high-quality carpets will have a deep, dense surface pile. Bend the edge; backing should "grin" through only slightly.

PADDING

Finally, you will need padding (also known as underlay or cushion) under your carpeting to add extra luxury underfoot and prolong the life of the rug. You will find padding made of cattle hair, jute-and-cattle hair, rubberized hair, or foam or sponge rubber. Some carpets come with a backing of bonded sponge or foam rubber which takes the place of underlay.

HARDWARE: THE HANG OF IT

There's nothing hard about hardware except its name. In fact, it's often the hardware that makes window dressing easy—there's a rod that will bend, curve or custom-fit around every window problem. And for every rod, there are clever little brackets, screws and etceteras to help it do the job better for your particular window. Bay, bow, arch, cathedral—all the answers are prepackaged and waiting on your drapery dealer's counter. Or in his special-order book, which means he can custom measure and design hardware for any application under your roof.

In fact, once you realize the wealth of hardware available today, it's often possible for you to custom-design your own, right from the ready-made counter, with less cost and delay than going through the dealer. For example, extender sections can stretch old rods to fit new, wider windows; new brackets that accommodate an extra rod will let you hang double curtains in place of a single-layer treatment; extension brackets project old rods over a new air-conditioner.

Before you buy or order any hardware, it's essential to understand the anatomy of a window and how to take accurate measurements (below). For a proper fit, rods should be bought and installed before you measure for the window dressing itself. However, you must consider the eventual weight of the completed treatment when purchasing rods, most of which come in heavy-duty strengths. For extra-long, extra-heavy traverse draperies, electric rods are available that draw automatically at the touch of a switch installed anywhere in the room—or even in adjoining rooms.

ANATOMY OF A WINDOW

Here's the familiar double-hung window with movable sashes. Other windows may shape up differently, but the terms—frame, sash, sill, etc.—carry over in most cases. In any case, the three lengths shown here are proper for all window treatments: from the top of the frame to the sill, to the apron bottom, and to the floor, where draperies are usually hemmed to clear the rug (they may touch the floor).

When measuring for hardware, use a metal tape and always take individual dimensions for each window—they only *look* alike. Remember to include the side returns and center overlap in estimates for drapery fabric. Depending on the treatment you choose, rods may be installed on the ceiling, on the wall, or on the window frame itself.

Hardware can be as attractive as it is functional, often adding decorative new dimensions to the window treatment you choose. Look for rods designed to be seen as well as used, rods that fit your overall window theme.

Wrought iron adapts beautifully to a Mediterranean mood; antiqued brass is right for any classic window dress; handsome wood rods can be bought already finished or ready to paint to pick up any color in your curtains. Wood and metal rings are also available for completely coordinated treatments. Many traverse rods have ornamental "rings" already attached, so you can combine looks with the convenience of automatic drawing. In addition to rods, there are decorative end supports, and many styles of handsome hold-backs, plus other hardware accessories that work equally hard behind-the-scenes (see the opposite page).

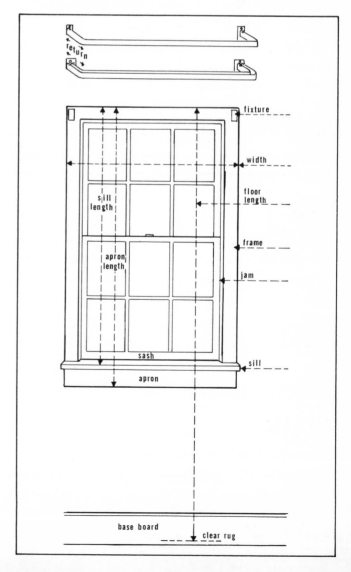

INSTALLMENT PLAN

Hardware plays a triple role in hanging window dressings: (1) There's the kind of hardware that holds the rod to the wall, (2) hardware that teams up with the rod, and (3) hardware that links the rod to curtains or draperies. Here is a short sampling of all three types, with examples chosen from among the many offerings your hardware dealer displays. In most cases pre-packaged rods will come complete with any special trappings they require, but a working knowledge of what's available can help you make the most of old rods and draperies when adapting them to your new windows.

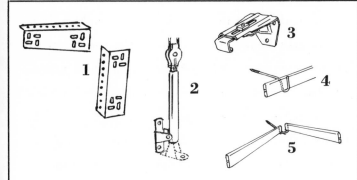

Hardware for rods: (1) Extender plates mount to window frame, rod mounts to them for wider, taller look. (2) Tension pulley holds traverse cords taut for easy draw, attaches to wall or floor. (3) Support bracket for single traverse rod keeps draperies from sagging (also comes double). (4) Support hook for single curtain rod (available for double rod). (5) Angle support for single rods that meet in a corner.

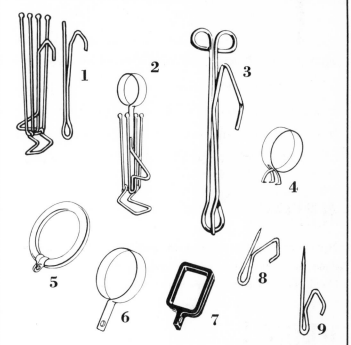

Hardware for curtains: From among the dozens of drapery rings and hooks available, here are samples of the most useful types. Each comes in different sizes, weights and finishes to meet your special need, so take time to search out exactly the right one. (1) Nip-Tite Ceiling Hook and End Pin for use with Conso Bestpleat pleater tape. (2) Nip-Tite Pleater Ring for cafes (use with Bestpleat). (3) Empire Slip-On Drapery Hook slips into pleats of ready-made draperies. (4) Clip-on ring for cafe curtains. (5) Round ring with short shank. (6) Long shank ring. (7) Decorative square ring. (8) Short Pin Sharp Hook and (9) Long Pin Sharp Hook.

Hardware for walls: Don't rely on ordinary wood screws to hold rods when you're installing them outside the window frame into plaster, masonry or sheet rock walls. Reach instead for (1) wall plug or (2) plaster screw for plaster walls, (3) toggle bolt or (4) molly bolt for sheet rock walls. They flare open (see 5) and can't work loose in hollow walls.

POINTS TO REMEMBER

- Rods should overlap at least 10″ in the center to prevent sagging. To be sure, buy the next longest rod.

- Nails are no good for any but the lightest, never-touched window treatments. Use screws instead, and never try to work them into the miter joint of the window casing. They will quickly work loose again.

- Don't fail to add both side returns on rods when you measure for draperies. Also allow for a 3″ overlap in the center when draperies traverse.

- Plan so top of drapery when installed conceals top of window frame. Hems should clear rug or floor by ½″ for easy drawing.

FABRICS DEFINED

Until some 60 years ago, everything in which we dressed ourselves and our homes came almost directly from Mother Nature. Cotton, wool, silk and linen were all there was to be woven into fabrics. Then science reached into some unlikely places to pull out some most likable new fibers—fibers made from coal, petroleum, salt and water, even air, woven into fabrics that won't wrinkle, won't rot, won't let you iron them even if you want to.

The world currently uses more than eight million tons of man-made fibers each year. But sometimes we use them without really understanding which fabrics give back the most for the money and why. Some nineteen man-made fibers are officially recognized by the Federal Trade Commission. Below is a thumbnail sketch of those most often found in home furnishings:

ACETATE

Made into supple fabrics with good drapability, pleasing hand, resistance to wrinkling and fading. Often found in blends with other fibers for drapery materials and upholstery.

ACRYLIC

Known for light weight, warmth, durability and soft hand. Has excellent shape retention—resists sagging, stretching and wrinkling. Found in drapery and upholstery materials, carpeting, blankets and fleece fabrics.

GLASS

True ease of maintenance in curtains, bedspreads, tablecloths, draperies — no ironing allowed. Strong, virtually fade-proof and stretch-proof, resistant to heat, flame, most chemicals. Made into upholstery fabric, it can take abrasion, resists stains (without additional treatment) and seldom fuzzes.

MODACRYLIC

Fabrics made from modacrylic fibers are resilient, flame-resistant and shape retentive. Found in draperies, curtains.

NYLON

Noted for great strength, dyeability and smooth, soft hand. Its splendid resistance to abrasion makes it an upholstery favorite, where it may be combined with other fibers. You will find upholstery materials tagged "nylon warp," where only part of the weave is nylon, or "100 per cent nylon pile," or "nylon face," both of which mean that the wearing surface is made entirely of nylon. It is also important for draperies, curtains, bedspreads. Stretch nylon has made possible upholstery fabrics that cling like skin.

OLEFIN

(Polypropylene)—Strong and lightweight, extremely resistant to fading, moisture and, therefore, stains. Used in upholstery fabrics and slipcovers.

POLYESTER

Very durable, stretch- and shrink-resistant. Naturally crisp, a favorite for sheer curtains. Often found in blends.

POLYURETHANE (or URETHANE)

Durable, easy-care plastic fabric that can assume a variety of appearances, from wet-look vinyl to suede with a kid glove feel.

RAYON

Oldest man-made fiber and second only to cotton in use for home fashions. Exceptionally colorfast (when solution dyed) and very versatile. Found in fabrics for draperies, slipcovers, curtains, upholstery, tablecloths, sheets, bedspreads.

MAN-MADE SUEDE

Actually man-made from synthetic film to resemble suede leather. Upholstery fabrics have soft, doeskin-like texture, are highly stain-resistant, waterproof, clean with soap and water.

VINYL

Not a fiber as such, but an extremely tough, easy-to-clean fabric made of plastic. Long billed as a "practical" material, now gone high fashion for shower curtains, wallcoverings, upholstery, where it can take many forms, from looking "wet" to emulating fine, soft leather. It can also be woven into porous fabrics called "poromerics." High-quality vinyls are backed with cloth and urethane foam.

Almost all these fibers, plus the natural ones, will be found woven into an extensive variety of fabrics. And choosing the right one for the right role often depends as much on how the weaving is done as on the fiber used, since weave determines both appearance and durability. For example, any number of fibers may be woven into tweeds, velvets or damasks, but some will be suitable for curtains, some for draperies, others for slipcovers and upholstery, depending on the weight of the material and the tightness of the weave. Before you buy, evaluate both the job you want the fabric to do and the way you want it to look while it's doing that job, then follow this general guide:

FOR GLASS CURTAINS:

Choose sheer fabrics such as voile or organdy, preferably in drip-dry fibers, in white or pale tints.

FOR UNLINED DRAPERIES:

Light- or medium-weight fabrics with either an open weave or opaque quality, for example, monk's cloth, homespun, muslin, chintz. Since there is no protective lining, sun-fastness is important. So is abrasion-resistance if they draw.

FOR LINED DRAPERIES:

Fabric weight depends on drapery length—medium-weight for cafes or sill-length, heaviest for full-length. Choose fabric that will not stretch or sag, e.g., velvet, chintz, damask.

FOR SLIPCOVERS AND UPHOLSTERY:

Very tightly woven fabrics, heaviest and tightest for upholstery—if you can see light through the fabric it is too short-lived for upholstery. For durability, choose textured rather than smooth surfaces, quilted rather than plain chintz, and look for protective stain-resistant finishes. For elegance, brocades, satins, velvets and velours still abound and, with the new fibers and finishes, you don't have to sacrifice longevity to enjoy them. For more informal rooms, look to tight tweeds, denims, vinyls, etc.

RESILIENT FLOORS: WHAT'S NEW UNDERFOOT

Decorating took a giant step forward when resilient floors were invented. Up till then, we had clumped around on rigid surfaces — wood, brick, elegant-but-cold marble. Resilient flooring, as its name implies, offers some springiness underfoot. And along with the added comfort and quiet, it offers a whole new world of good looks and easy upkeep, including products that preclude waxing forever.

Under the genus *Resilient Floors* come many different species, including both man-made and natural materials, square tiles and larger sheet goods. There's something to suit every taste, every budget and every room in the house, from the kitchen, where resilient floors have always reigned, into the most elegant of living rooms. Which does, indeed, prove how far such floors have climbed the social ladder. Not too long ago, lowly linoleum, forefather of all resilient flooring, was usually found in the pantry, kitchen, back hallway.

Deservedly so, since its styling was equally unglamorous. Time and technology have changed all that. Today you can buy "marble" by the roll, "brick" by the yard; you can have handsome Moorish "tile" or realistic "wood" squares comfortably backed with foam.

In fact, your choice of floors is really limited only by your bank account and by the location of the room you're revitalizing. Depending on the type of subfloor, the kind of backing the flooring has, and the kind of adhesive used, some products are meant to go *below grade* (in rooms below ground level); some go *on grade* (at ground level); some *above grade* (suspended at least 18 inches above ventilated air space). See the accompanying chart. Some products are meant for heavy traffic, others for less busy areas. Some should be installed by professionals, others have the do-it-yourselfer in mind. The guide below will help you decide on the right resilient flooring:

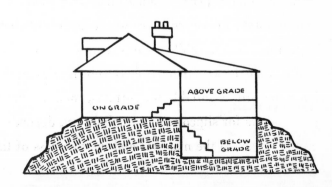

TILES vs. SHEET GOODS

Tiles are usually 9-inch or 12-inch squares, which facilitates installing them yourself. Many patterns are now made with adhesive backing you simply peel and stick down. Sheet goods generally come in rolls 6- to 12-feet wide; may be loose-laid or cemented down permanently for seamless, easy-to-clean floors.

ASPHALT TILE

Least expensive and least versatile. Resists alkali so is good for basements, laundry areas, etc., but oil and grease are its natural enemies.

CONTINUOUS FLOORING

See Poured Floors.

CORK TILE

Natural material in a pleasant range of brown tones. Now usually protected with a clear plastic finish to offer some resistance to stains, dents. Comfortable and quiet underfoot.

CUSHIONED VINYL

Sheet goods with long-wearing vinyl surface and bonded-on backing layer of foam. Very soft and sound-absorbing.

EMBOSSED SURFACES

Relief work which adds realistic depth to surface designs, producing "bricks," "wood grains," etc. you can actually feel.

INLAID VINYL

Design is inlaid in solid vinyl wear surface so it goes all the way through. Costs more but lasts longer than roto, or printed, vinyl, especially in heavily traveled areas.

LINOLEUM

Old flooring standby brought up-to-date with new materials and designs. Economical, sturdy and easy to maintain, but usually less durable than some of the vinyl products. You will find that it bears little resemblance to the "kitchen" linoleum of olden times.

POURED FLOORS

A relatively new concept in resilient flooring where a layer of polyurethane is spread over the subfloor, topped with thin vinyl acetate chips, then covered with a wear surface of clear polyurethane. Produces seamless, easy-to-keep floors. Variations on this method can be used almost anywhere and the finished design can be rigidly controlled.

ROTOVINYL (or PRINTED VINYL)

Design is rotogravure-printed on felt or asbestos backing, topped with clear vinyl film. When protective film wears away, design follows quickly. Low costs makes it practical for low-traffic areas.

RUBBER TILE

Extremely comfortable underfoot, durable and resistant to dents, but demands diligent upkeep.

VINYL ASBESTOS

Combination of vinyl and asbestos in long-wearing, medium-priced, well-styled tiles which offer an excellent buy for most flooring needs.

VINYL

Most durable and most expensive resilient flooring material. Stain-resistant, easy to maintain, available in a vast range of designs. See also Cushioned Vinyl, Inlaid Vinyl and Rotovinyl.

THE FRINGE AREAS ARE EVERYWHERE

Trimmings are the time-honored finishing touches to every well-dressed interior, the "accessories" of home fashions. And like the accessories of women's fashion, they can do wonders for the rest of an "outfit." Use them in the obvious places—on pillows, tablecloths, curtains, draperies, slipcovers and rugs. But don't overlook the subtle touches trimmings can provide elsewhere—around a molding or window frame, as picture matting, etc.

Just be sure you are *subtle*. Over-lavish layers of fringe went out with the Victorian age. Trimmings today are fresh and bright, in strong, new colors as well as traditional favorites, in modern fibers that marry well with all the new fabrics. Major trim designers have kept pace with the movement toward modern living, producing bold, wide woven braids and fringes to suit the sleekest settings.

But if you still love Early American or formal French, you can find complementary cotton pompons or elegant silky tassels to your taste. There's trimming for every room, every mood, every application. They come in a myriad of sizes, colors, fibers and styles. Here's a brief rundown to help you choose from among the many exciting offerings you'll find at your dealer's:

TRIMMING STYLES

There are four major categories into which most trimmings fit: (1) Those with decorative headings which are meant to show when applied, for example, to draperies; (2) Weltings which are inserted in the seams of a slipcover or pillow; (3) Trimmings with decorative headings that are flat enough to conceal in a seam if you prefer, e.g., moss fringe; (4) Flat, decorative braids, great for pillows, slipcovers, towels, etc. Under these four general groupings fall thousands of different trimmings. Among the more basic and popular types:

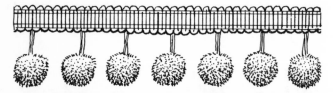

A. BALL FRINGE—Fluffy pompons attached to a woven heading, sometimes combined with yarn scallops.

B. BRAIDS—Flat trimmings woven the same on both edges. Available in many widths (usually two-to-four inches) and in many styles, from elegant to classic to contemporary.

C. GIMP—Narrow ornamental trim in rayon or cotton.

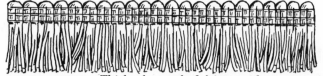

D. MOSS FRINGE—Thick, short-tufted fringe with a narrow, tailored heading.

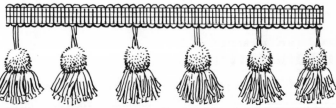

E. BALL-TASSEL FRINGE—Combination ball-and-tassel attached to a tailored heading.

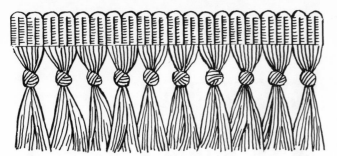

F. KNOTTED FRINGE—Grouped strands of yarn knotted near a woven heading.

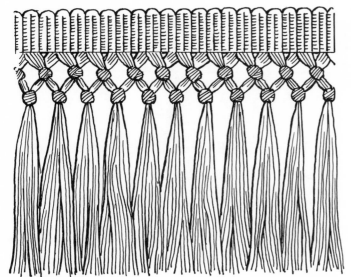

G. DOUBLE-KNOTTED FRINGE—Two rows of knotting near the heading.

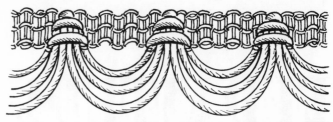

H. RAT-TAIL FRINGE—Sleek garlands of rayon cord swagged to a woven heading.

I. TASSEL FRINGE—Tassels attached by thread loops to a woven heading.

TRIMMING FIBERS

Although the majority of trimmings your dealer carries are made of cotton or rayon, you will also find wool fringes for rugs, jute trimmings for contemporary designs and acrylic trimmings for use with permanent press fabrics. The trimming fiber is usually but not always matched to the fabric on which it's going, i.e., cotton and spun rayon trimmings on cotton and other washable fabrics, rayon trimmings on fabrics you plan to dry-clean. Wool trim should also be dry-cleaned. Any trimming with "Vat Dyed" on its label can be washed, but since some shrinkage is almost certain, take care to ease the trim on loosely when sewing it to fabric. Or pre-shrink it by washing both trim and fabric separately before sewing (trim should always be pre-shrunk when used on fiber glass fabrics).

TRIMMING USES

Almost anywhere, to perk up a color scheme, coordinate, add emphasis and interest—as long as it's not overdone. For the most decorating impact, repeat a trimming at least twice in a room, once prominently, once more subtly. You may try using the same trimming in different sizes, especially effective with some of the flat braids. Remember, too, that trimmings are the perfect way to introduce your brightest accent into a color scheme. Unless you're an expert, don't mix too many styles, too many colors of trimmings in one room, and do try to keep the styles and colors you choose in harmony with your overall decorating mood:

FORMAL ROOMS are the natural setting for silky tassels, gimps, rat-tail fringes, lustrous braids, used on draperies, slipcovers, pillows.

CASUAL ROOMS take to ball fringes, moss fringe, ball-tassel fringes in bouncy colors, knotted fringes on bedspreads and bright cotton braids anywhere.

MODERN ROOMS call for some of the exciting new superbraids, up to four inches wide in smashing colors, wood molds and clear crystals on tailored headings, applied at windows, on pillows, even to the walls.

FURNITURE STYLES AND QUALITY

The history of furniture is the story of mankind. Perhaps more than any of the arts and crafts, the furniture of the past reveals how man really lived, behind the closed doors of his own home as well as in the public eye. How comfortably he sat, slept and stored his belongings parallels the evolution of civilization. As man mastered his external environment, he conquered inner space, too, and refined its furnishings from crude necessities into true works of art.

The process was a long and fascinating one that really begins in the small hours of history and still makes "antiquing" such popular sport today. History, however, has not been physically kind to household furnishings, most of which were made of perishable wood. Except for the furniture that occasionally appears in ancient works of art, and treasures from the tombs of Egypt, where the climate literally embalmed the pieces, the recorded history of furniture begins fairly recently, with the Greeks and Romans.

No matter, really, to today's interior designer interested in period furnishings. For until the Renaissance of the 15th century, household comforts were actually very limited. The Greeks had chairs, stools, couches, tables and chests, and that was about all, a far cry from the specialized clutter that makes our lives so convenient today. Things got even bleaker during the Middle Ages when so many people were hopelessly poor and political unrest turned rich nobles into nomads. To keep guard over their domains, they had to move constantly from house to house, taking all their valuables along. Furniture, therefore, was designed to be mobile—either it came apart to be packed into trunks or was sturdy enough to travel on horseback.

Such a climate, naturally, did not foster an emphasis on furniture. We're told that even the richest castles seldom had more than two chairs, and they were reserved for the master and one important guest. Everyone else sat on rough benches or stools. Even today, "The Chairman" still sits in the position of authority at official gatherings.

Then came the Renaissance, all kinds of luxurious things began to happen in people's homes, and furniture began to take the forms we still cherish half a millenium later.

And it's at this point that today's decorators begin to

take interest. Renaissance furniture is generally too rich, too elaborate and too large for modern homes, but it signaled the rebirth of interest in interiors, and spawned many of the succeeding styles we still find so appealing so many years later.

A brief guide to those styles follows, plus a chronological chart that shows what was happening concurrently in the countries whose tastes have touched ours the most: France, England and, of course, earlier America. While every country has developed its own furniture styles, just as every country has its national dress and special foods, American interior design today draws most heavily on these three sources. Others become the accent pieces, the spices that add interest to the rest of the room. Mediterranean furniture is an obvious exception to this generalization, although "Mediterranean" itself is a word coined to cover the modern, machine-made versions of a style inspired by all the countries around the Mediterranean Sea.

Strictly speaking, "period" furniture means a style popular during a certain period of the past. And, in most cases, that means antiques, defined officially by the U.S. Customs Department as one hundred years old or more. Practically speaking, however, only the *inspiration* for the pieces need come from the past, since most of the actual antiques are behind museums' velvet ropes or tucked away in the homes of the very, very wealthy. The rest of us can be quite content with modern versions of the old masterpieces, versions which, in many instances, have been scaled to modern rooms and adapted to modern manufacturing methods and materials.

Such refinements (as long as they are rendered with a discerning hand) make the past more likable and more livable for the present, without disturbing the overall effect. Only an historian could love a room strictly recreated from yesteryear, point by painstaking point, then fixed in amber for admiration only. That's not decorating — that's collecting, and calls more for scholarship than taste. Decorating is a *living* art.

Still, the traditionalists can have their favorite period rooms and live in them, too. The trick, as we've pointed out often before, is to recreate the *spirit* of the period, not the letter. Look again at pages 12 and 13, then mate one of those moods with the furniture style that suits you best from the coming eight pages. The capsule histories will help you get the feel of the period that produced each style, whether it was the upperclass elegance of the French Louis' or the spartan lives of the American settlers. To fully appreciate the furniture of a time, you must understand the time itself. In the process, however, don't fall victim to stratified thinking. Most of the names and dates assigned to the various periods are somewhat arbitrary. The ruling monarch often lent his name to the fashions of his day . . . and often with good reason in the days when the Court set the pace for the rest of the country.

Still, we would be misleading you if we didn't point out that evolution is the key word here. While it is convenient to be able to put period labels on furniture styles for the purpose of reference, these styles don't begin and end at set times in history. They evolve slowly from the styles that have preceded them until they become absorbed into ensuing fashions.

Most of the styles discussed here have been selected because their beauty, charm or craftsmanship have won them a permanent place in mankind's history . . . and in his home.

FRENCH

LOUIS XIV

France was already on the rise, both politically and artistically, when Louis XIV came to the throne in 1643, determined to make his country the center of the arts. He filled France with artisans imported from all over Europe and directed their energies to glorifying his reign. He became "The Sun King," indeed, and the splendor of Versailles dazzled the rest of the world. Aubusson carpets, Gobelins tapestries and the great marquetry work of André Charles Boulle flourished under Louis' direction. Furnishings were baroque in every sense of the word: sumptuous, heroic, massive, richly ornamented—generally too much so for today's taste, and today's smaller-scaled rooms.

LOUIS XV

The period known as the Regency (or Régence) spanned the time from Louis XIV's death in 1715 till his grandson was old enough to take over as Louis XV in 1723. Artistically, the era was marked by a softening of Louis XIV's masculine grandiosity into the gentle, feminine style that came to be known as rococo under Louis XV. Small-scaled where Louis XIV had been grand, intimate where its predecessor had been forbodingly formal, soft and grayed in colors where it had been vibrant and clear, the Louis XV style is a harmony of flowing lines. Look for asymmetry above all, chinoiserie, the cabriole leg and the emergence of the *chaise longue* and *bergère*, both designed for the comfort of the sitter.

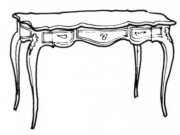

LOUIS XVI

Eventually, of course, everyone grew tired of those never-ending curves and frills. Even before Louis XV died in 1774, French taste was tending back toward the straight line. So when Pompeii and Herculaneum were unearthed in 1755, a new vogue for ancient restraints and classic ornamentation surfaced along with them. Furniture legs went back to being straight and architectural. Decorative motifs were symmetrical and borrowed from the ancients—egg-and-dart, laurel and acanthus, lyres, festoons, etc. Plain panels, perhaps with delicate borders, became popular. So did toiles de Jouy and oval-backed chairs, often topped with a bowknot.

DIRECTOIRE

From the chaos of the French Revolution emerged a transitional government and a transitional style, both known as the Directoire and neither complete unto itself. The government of the Directors lasted for four years, from 1795-1799, while Napoleon gathered strength for his coup d'etat. And during that time the Directoire style moved the lyric classicism of the Louis XVI era toward the full-blown, austere formality of the Empire Period. Following the lead of the artist Jacques Louis David, Directoire furniture closely emulated classical forms, superimposed with revolutionary symbols—fasces, arrows, pikes, etc.

EMPIRE

Just as he galvanized the shaky state of France into a world power, Napoleon pulled all the arts together into the Empire style, literally by commanding it. Two unknown young architects named Percier and Fontaine were assigned to create a style to glorify the new empire, and they went about it by reaching straight back into antiquity. The furnishings they dictated from 1801-1815 were massive and architectural, absolutely symmetrical and generally devoid of carving except for gilt bronze mounts in the form of military and ancient symbols. Look also for Napoleon's famous initial and his symbol, the bee. Concurrent with Napoleon's rise came the development of the machine, which kept spreading the style even after Waterloo in 1815.

PROVINCIAL

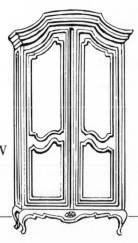

The new styles invented by the French kings and their courtiers didn't escape the notice of the lesser folk in the provinces away from Paris. As early as the 17th century, the bourgeoisie and peasantry began to acquire sufficient wealth to afford their own versions of what was popular at Court. Created by local craftsmen, the copies were charmingly crude compared to their royal prototypes and generally made in solid native woods without lavish embellishment. The Louis XV style of the 18th century is the most characteristic provincial style. Look also for straw-bottomed chairs, chintz, pewter, faience, armoires and the unique *lit clos*.

ENGLISH

THE EARLY PERIODS

The various styles of English furniture owe as much to the woods from which they were made as they do to the political periods in which they appeared. For example, the Age of Oak extends through a succession of 16th- and 17th-century rulers, survives Cromwell and the Puritan Commonwealth, and runs into the time when the monarchy was restored. A native wood, oak was extremely hard and difficult to carve, hence the heavy, massive, almost crudely rendered furniture of the Early Periods (including Tudor, Elizabethan and early Jacobean). Huge, bulbous-melon legs appeared everywhere, braced with low, square stretchers. As the effects of the Italian Renaissance spread northward, the earlier Gothic motifs gradually gave way to Romayne work (carvings inspired by Rome) and other classical designs. Cromwell and the Puritans ruled over a period or undecorated austerity (1649-60). But with the restoration of Charles II, foreign influences began to be felt, walnut appeared, and baroque richness flowered.

WILLIAM and MARY

They came to the throne in 1688, bringing the baroque style with them full-blown from Holland. England blossomed with richly carved and turned furniture, complete with elaborate marquetry, veneers, lacquer and japanning. Most typical of the William and Mary style are legs with trumpet, bell, cup and bun turnings, braced with serpentine stretchers which are often topped at the intersection with a vase-shaped finial. The so-called Spanish foot, which looks like an inward-curling hand resting on its knuckles, is also a hallmark. Walnut continued to be the dominant wood.

QUEEN ANNE

Historians have it that Queen Anne was neither interested nor influential in the development of the elegant, refined furniture style that bears her name. Nonetheless, her reign, from (1702-14) saw the English penchant for calm and reserve transferred to furnishings, gradually transforming the exuberant baroque of the preceding periods into controlled curves and gently carved surfaces. Emphasis began to shift to the understated beauty of unadorned woods, and the simple, splat-back chair appeared. The most prevailing characteristic of the period is the cabriole leg, which was often carved on the knee with scallop-shell motifs and often ended in club or ball-and-claw feet.

GEORGIAN

CHIPPENDALE

Four Georges ruled England from 1714 to 1830, and during this time some of the greatest names in furniture making rose to lasting fame. Thomas Chippendale led the era with the publication of "The Gentleman and Cabinet-Maker's Director" in 1754, which immediately made him the tastesetter for all of England and abroad. His style, worked mainly in mahogany, included elements of the rococo, the Gothic and Chinese, all rendered with masculine directness and strength.

ADAM

The Adam brothers, Robert and James, spread the classicism unearthed at Pompeii and Herculaneum into virtually every phase of English interior design from about 1762-1794. Their furniture is symmetrical in both form and ornament, supported on straight legs, and so finely scaled the pieces sometimes appear delicate. Satinwood became a favorite.

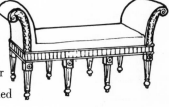

HEPPLEWHITE

George Hepplewhite took the Adams' neo-classic influences and refined them first into subtle curves, then into graceful, elegant pieces with tapered, straight legs. Chairs were his masterpieces, rendered in five back styles: oval, wheel, heart, shield and camel, always filled with delicately carved splats. Satinwood and painted furniture are other characteristics of Hepplewhite, whose "Cabinetmakers' and Upholsterers' Guide" kept up his influence long after he died in 1786.

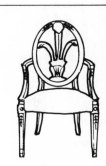

SHERATON

Also the author of a book on furniture styles, Thomas Sheraton ranks with Chippendale and Hepplewhite as an 18th-century great. His light, almost fragile designs are based primarily on all straight lines and geometric symmetry. Chair backs are always square.

REGENCY

George, Prince of Wales, acted as Regent of England from 1811-1820, and the Regency produced a style of its own. At first following the French Directoire and Empire styles, furniture makers sought to copy exactly the pieces excavated from ancient sources. However, the trend quickly fell into half-archeological, half-fanciful creations, characterized by flat planes and slender shapes. Other Regency influences came from the continuing interest in Chinese and Gothic motifs.

AMERICAN

EARLY AMERICAN

This is a difficult style to pin down to a certain segment of time, because it represents the earliest efforts of American settlers to create furniture on the demanding frontier. And that frontier kept moving westward from 1607 through the 19th century. In the main, however, Early American has come to mean the charming—if somewhat crude—furnishings made by the country's original settlers along the Eastern Seaboard (1607-1720). Most of them came from England and most of their furnishings followed what they remembered of the Tudor, Elizabethan and Jacobean styles they left behind. But the new versions were built of native woods, pine, cherry and maple, and boasted only crude ornamentation. Contemporary renditions of Early American tend to be sturdy and simple, with turned legs, brass or iron hardware and abundant scallops.

COLONIAL

The period leading up through the American Revolution (1720-1781) became very comfortable for many of the American colonists. England was enjoying the great Georgian period of furniture, and wealthy settlers from Virginia to New England knew and wanted what was in vogue at home. Direct importation was limited, so American craftsmen armed themselves with guidebooks like Chippendale's "Director" and set about turning out native treasures. Along the way, they added uniquely American characteristics, e.g., the block front and the imposing highboy on its tall legs. Boston, Newport and Philadelphia became centers for furniture making, and their products compared handsomely with the English works they sought to emulate.

FEDERAL

Once the Federal Government was established in 1789, America tried to turn her back on English influence by reverting to Greek and Roman styles. The influence of the French Directoire style touched America briefly and produced a master in Duncan Phyfe. Spread eagles, stars and stripes, etc., also characterize the Federal period, which later, during the Empire phase, fell victim to the heavy, stolid styles inspired by the French Empire.

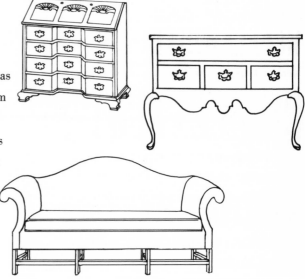

DUNCAN PHYFE

An immigrant from Scotland, Phyfe first learned cabinetmaking in Albany, New York. Then, about 1790, he opened the New York City shop that won him almost instant fame. He was the primary exponent of the American Directory style, inspired by what was happening in France and England at the end of the 18th century. Sheraton's styles appealed to him particularly. In fact, Sheraton literally monopolized American furniture making from 1795 until 1820, and many of the finest pieces in the style were created by Phyfe. However, he added his own dimension of greatness to his interpretations, working in mahogany and satinwood with exquisite delicacy of line and detail. Slender and light in scale, Phyfe's designs were almost Grecian in their simplicity. He favored such classical motifs as the acanthus leaf and curving X-form legs for chairs, stools and settees, and produced couches freely adapted from the so-called Récamier lounge made famous by David in France. Among the typical features of the Phyfe school are pedestal supports for tables with concave, flared legs; fine lines of reeding on the frames for chairs and sofas; cornucopia legs or legs ending in stylized animal feet. His chairs are noted for their elegant, lyre-shaped splats. Phyfe kept working until 1854, but his later creations—which he himself called ugly—were in the massive Empire style, a degeneration forced by competition with machine-made furniture.

19th CENTURY

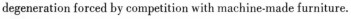

Turning into the 19th century, America confronted a free-for-all in matters of style. She was not alone—after the French Empire and English Regency, recognizable styles dissolved into a mishmash from which were pulled, at various times, revived versions of the Gothic, the Romanesque, the Renaissance, the Grecian, Louis XVI and others. The new versions burst forth with more of everything than their prototypes —more curves, more arches, more elaborate carvings. By the time the Victorian era officially arrived in midcentury, the Machine Age was already in high gear, spreading these exaggerations to every parlor in the country. Or nearly so. There are several pauses in the flow of florid designs. Shaker furniture, actually begun when the communal religious sect was founded in the late 1700's, is still admired for its simplicity and craftsmanship. Also popular still are Hitchcock chairs, based on Sheraton Empire designs and first machine-produced by Lambert Hitchcock in 1818. Usually painted black with stenciled designs, they're still made and widely sold today. Mission furniture, a late 19th- early 20th-century creation inspired by Spanish missions in the Southwest, did not fare so well, despite its comparative simplicity. Lacking the charm of the originals, the reproductions were heavy, square, upholstered with leather and exposed nailheads.

OTHER STYLES

MEDITERRANEAN

Unless written in the past few years, no furniture dictionary would include the term "Mediterranean." The word has been coined by the furniture profession to describe the whole range of designs inspired by the countries around the Mediterranean Sea, particularly Spain. Lately, influences from other Spanish-speaking countries such as Peru and Mexico have been absorbed into the style, which is generally distinguished by its grand scale, emphasis on wood with heavy carvings and touches of wrought iron and leather.

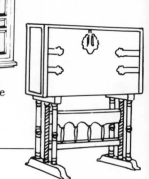

BIEDERMEIER

Early 19th-century Austria had a favorite cartoon character called Papa Biedermeier, a rather stout country gentleman who was fond of comfort and of expressing uninformed opinions about many subjects. The furniture style that bears his name was derived from the French Empire but was well plumped for comfort. Sturdy, squarish and often humorously decorated, this was the somewhat charming style of the bourgeoisie.

ITALIAN

Italy gave us the Renaissance, and in so doing, won herself an honored place in the history of all the arts. Massive, dignified and imposing, Renaissance furniture of the 16th century looked back to ancient Rome for inspiration. In turn, artists of other countries looked to it. Eventually, in the mid-17th century, Louis XIV succeeded in shifting the center of artistic activity to France, and Italy became the imitator. Though greatly admired, most Italian Renaissance and baroque styles are too heroic, both in size and scope, for today's interiors.

ORIENTAL

Although the abundance of furniture known in the Western World does not exist in the East, the Orient has had a profound influence on interiors since Marco Polo's time. Chinoiserie, japanning, bamboo motifs, etc. are traceable through almost all styles, in almost all countries. Often it was the spirit of Oriental furniture, rather than the actual form of it, that inspired designers in the West, as during the late 19th-century rebellion against the elaborate horrors of Victorianism. In interior decorating today, Oriental accent pieces are especially compatible with most English period furniture, and with Modern, upon which it had a profound influence.

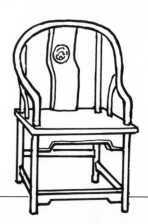

266

VICTORIAN

Invectives have been heaped upon the Victorian period nearly as profusely as its own florid ornamentation. And most of them are well-placed. Both in England and America, creative arts atrophied after the opening decades of the 19th century, and a public enamored with the Machine Age never demanded their revival. Instead, came revival after revival of earlier styles: Gothic, Turkish, Romanesque —anything, as long as it was novel. In the main, the Louis XV style was exaggerated into what we think of as "Victorian"—biscuit tufting, elaborate carving, horsehair and velvet upholstery, marble tops, etc., *small* touches of which can add interest to today's rooms.

ART NOUVEAU

Choking on the machine-made ornamentation and stale eclecticism of the Victorian era, artists began to rebel in the latter quarter of the 19th century. One of the most interesting products of their resurgence was L'Art Nouveau, literally, "New Art," which was based on the swirling forms of plant tendrils. The original Art Nouveau flourished from about 1895 until 1905, when it was absorbed into the whole movement toward Modern. Rediscovered in the late 1960's, it inspired a whole range of home fashions, from wallpapers and fabrics to a new vogue for Tiffany lamps.

MODERN

Architecture led the movement away from the extravaganzas of the Victorian age toward the clean, streamlined look we call "Modern." Furniture was right on its heels, since many of the outstanding architects in the early 20th century designed for the interiors as well as the exteriors of their buildings. Modern furniture is based on form; its design is determined by the purpose it serves; there are no frills, no excess ornamentation. The materials used in Modern reflect 20th-century technology: steel, glass, molded plastics, etc.

CONTEMPORARY

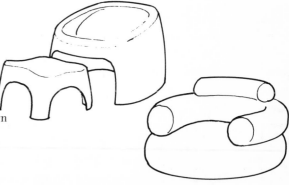

Contemporary is like the latest news bulletin in the history of furniture (of which Modern has already become an established chapter). As the name implies, Contemporary furniture is what's happening now. It's always new, often faddish, occasionally destined to take its place as a "traditional" Modern piece. Featuring new forms and new materials, Contemporary designs owe little allegiance to what's come before, leaning toward such innovations as stretch fabrics, inflatable vinyl and sculptured plastic foam.

FURNITURE FASHIONS THROUGH

	16th CENTURY	17th CENTURY	18th CENTURY

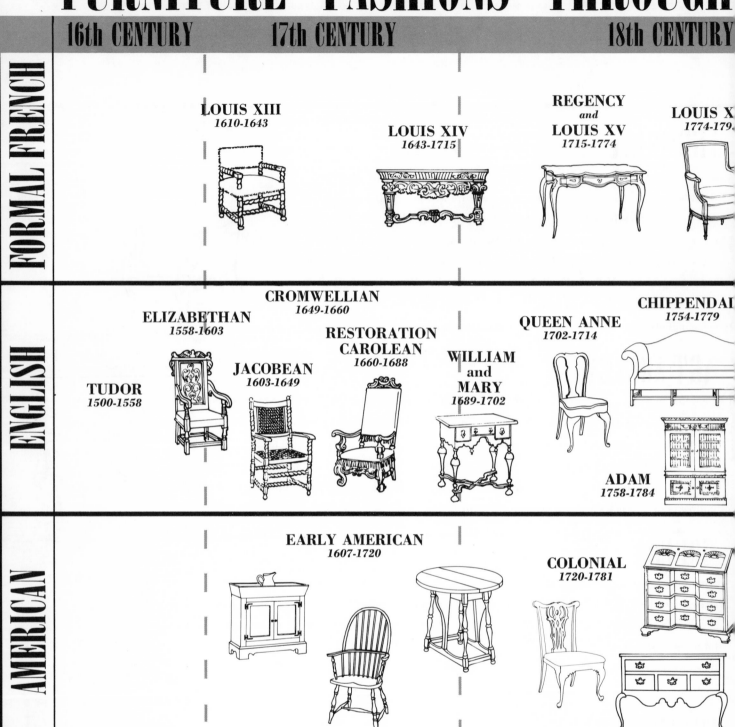

FORMAL FRENCH

LOUIS XIII
1610-1643

LOUIS XIV
1643-1715

REGENCY
and
LOUIS XV
1715-1774

LOUIS X
1774-179.

ENGLISH

CROMWELLIAN
1649-1660

ELIZABETHAN
1558-1603

RESTORATION
CAROLEAN
1660-1688

JACOBEAN
1603-1649

WILLIAM
and
MARY
1689-1702

QUEEN ANNE
1702-1714

CHIPPENDAI
1754-1779

TUDOR
1500-1558

ADAM
1758-1784

AMERICAN

EARLY AMERICAN
1607-1720

COLONIAL
1720-1781

OTHER STYLES

SPANISH
Still Influential in Mediterranean

ITALIAN
RENAISSANCE
15th and 16th Centuries

ORIENTAL
From Antiquity On

FRENCH PROVINCIAL
Primarily 18th Century
Still Popular

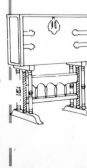

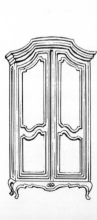

HISTORY

Traditional styles evolved as the world revolved, reflecting current events, contemporary tastes and, often, influences from other lands. This cross-centuries, cross-countries chart shows what was fashionable when and where.

19th CENTURY   20th CENTURY

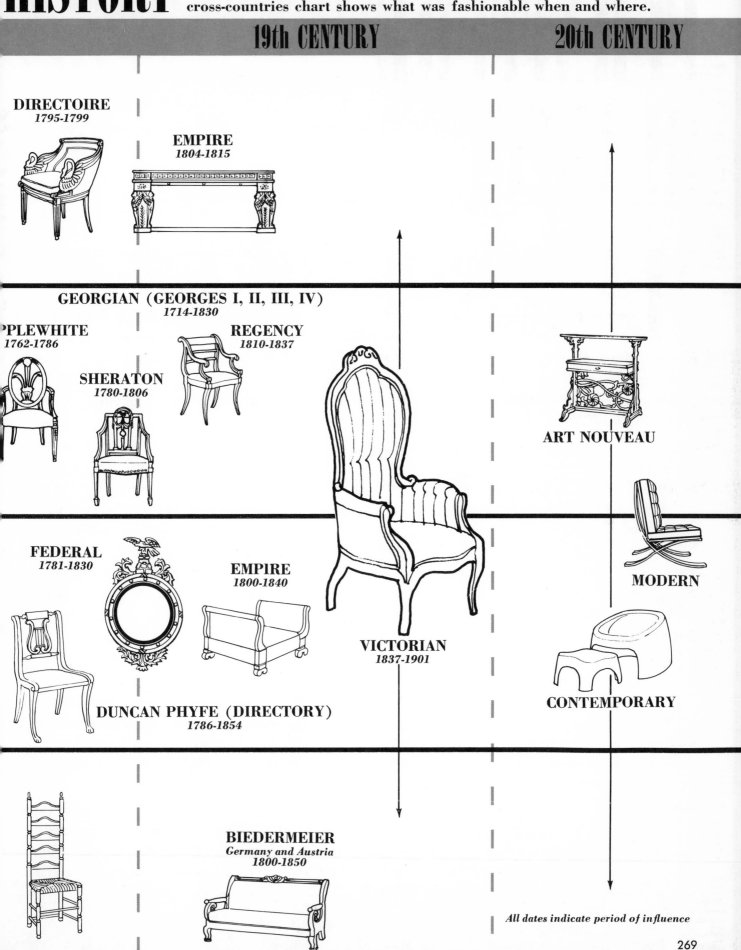

DIRECTOIRE
1795-1799

EMPIRE
1804-1815

GEORGIAN (GEORGES I, II, III, IV)
1714-1830

PPLEWHITE
1762-1786

SHERATON
1780-1806

REGENCY
1810-1837

ART NOUVEAU

FEDERAL
1781-1830

EMPIRE
1800-1840

VICTORIAN
1837-1901

MODERN

CONTEMPORARY

DUNCAN PHYFE (DIRECTORY)
1786-1854

BIEDERMEIER
Germany and Austria
1800-1850

All dates indicate period of influence

FURNITURE QUALITY

It takes more sense than dollars to buy quality in a piece of furniture. Cost alone does not indicate good or poor craftsmanship. You must learn to read between the lines on the price tag and develop an eye for the earmarks of well-made furniture, furniture you'll enjoy living with for a long, long time. An $18 desk lamp, sleekly designed for good light, is a quality product. A sofa that costs $500 is a poor purchase if you soon grow uncomfortable sitting upon or looking at it. High cost and quality aren't always synonymous, but good design and quality almost always are. Therefore, makers of quality furniture plan products that function as handsomely as they look.

Function therein becomes the first criterion by which you can judge quality in a piece of furniture. Will the piece perform its household duties well and be pleasing to look at in the process? Your eye becomes your biggest ally. Look the piece over carefully. Does its silhouette satisfy you? Is it properly proportioned for its setting? Inspect the finish carefully. Quality is lurking—or lacking—in little details. Are the corners smoothly joined on a desk, or is the gap merely closed with plastic wood? Is the welting on an upholstered chair tailored crisply and applied in a straight line? Does the fabric pattern match all the way around, and under the seat cushions where it doesn't even show? Does the wood graining match across the drawers of a dresser?

Your other senses are important in the process of judging quality, too. Feel the bottom of a dresser drawer with your fingertips. Will it be a safe place to store stockings and delicate lingerie? Handle the hardware. Is it heavy and solid, securely attached through the wood, or is it merely stamped out of metal? Twentieth-century ingenuity has given you another dimension to be aware of, though not necessarily wary—the fact that all which looks, feels and even knocks like wood often isn't. More and more components are molded from plastics to look exactly like the real thing, especially elaborately "carved" moldings on such ornate styles as Mediterranean. In general, the plastics are indistinguishable from wood. They are durable, and, above all, bring the handcarved look within budget range (although you'll find them on more expensive pieces too). Because some furniture salesmen fear past—and often unjust—prejudices against plastics they must be hard-pressed before they'll disclose the presence of such components. But you are entitled to know what you are buying, whether or not it really affects the appearance.

As you continue your search for clues to quality, pull out the drawers, swing open the doors and listen. They shouldn't stick, scrape or creak. Furniture that comes from the factory fitting poorly will grow worse with wear and varying humidity conditions in your home. Also beware of sofa springs that complain and chair legs that whine when you sit down. Furniture that talks back says bad things about the quality of its construction. Wise shoppers look *and* listen carefully to make sure their money is well spent.

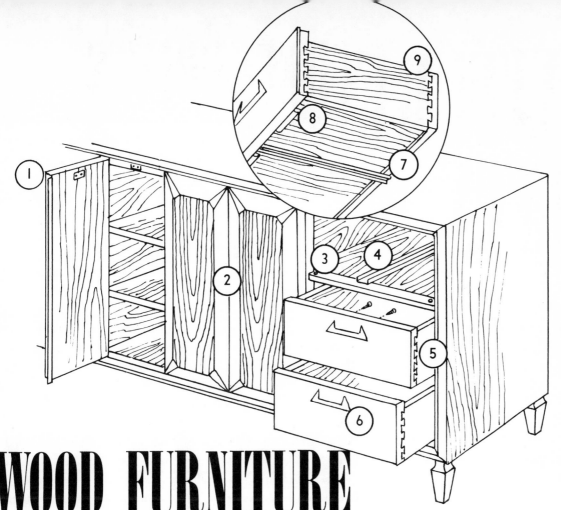

WOOD FURNITURE

(1) Interlocking door edges insure snug fit. (2) Graining is matched across front. (3) Small nylon tips, center glide (4) and glide on drawer (7) give quiet, smooth operation. Note also dust panels between drawers. Dovetailed joints front (5) and back (9) and reinforcing blocks at front (8) insure longevity. Pulls (6) are cast metal, securely attached through drawer front.

Quality in "case goods," as wood furniture is known, begins with the wood itself. Hardwood (wood from such leaf-bearing trees as mahogany, oak, walnut, pecan, etc., as opposed to softwood from evergreens) should be kiln-dried to prevent warping later. If you buy from a reputable manufacturer, you are assured that this important step has been taken. Don't, however, expect to find solid wood in the finished pieces, except perhaps in Colonial or Early American designs where it's historically accurate. Otherwise, only the legs, edges and other structural members of a piece will be cut from solid wood. More than 90 per cent of the furniture made today is veneer, wafer-thin sheets of hardwood laminated under heat and pressure to a center core of wood or wood product. Perfected by modern technology (although the technique is centuries old), veneering offers many advantages over solid woods: producing more exciting grain patterns, allowing matched grains on a single piece, and giving more strength than solid lumber several times its thickness. Because the veneers are applied with grains at angles to each other, the swelling, shrinking and splitting tendencies of solid wood are well controlled, allowing joints to be made tight, flush and smooth, sure signs of quality craftsmanship. Drawer construction is a candid measure of overall quality. Look for dovetailed joints, reinforcing blocks under the corners, and smooth operation. The wood need not match the exterior but should be smoothly finished. The back of a quality piece will also be finished as carefully as the front, with the panel recessed into the back and screwed on, not just nailed flush. Overall, the surface should be smooth to the touch, finished to enhance—not obscure—the natural grain.

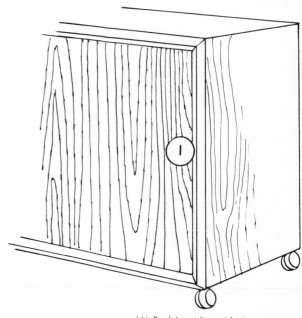

(1) Back is set in, not just nailed on, and is finished.

CHECKPOINTS

There's much more to quality furniture than meets the eye at first glance. Take a second, hard look behind and under the surface for the built-in features that insure a long working life for the piece of furniture and a happy purchase for you. Check any moving parts—hinges, table slides, etc.—carefully to see that they are made of heavy, sag-proof metal and function smoothly and noiselessly. On a piece with multiple doors make certain the hinges are precisely aligned or else the doors will hang and swing crookedly. Magnetic catches hidden inside are another desirable feature. On better pieces, glass panels in the doors will be set into the frame and anchored, rattleproof, behind strips of wood. Furniture of lesser quality uses a simple wood overlay to simulate the set-in look. Test the durability of case goods by attempting to rock them. If they wobble they are poorly made. Give chairs the same test by sitting in them and swaying from side to side. They won't rock if they're properly constructed on the bottom: legs cut from sturdy, smoothly grained wood and anchored securely by screwed-on wooden blocks in each corner. Legs on tables should be equally well braced. Another prime feature to watch for are self-leveling casters set into the feet of tables and case goods to keep them even on unlevel floors. Never buy an expansion table without first testing its operation. It should function easily enough for one person to handle. Also check to see that the wood and finish match on all the leaves. Here you may want to take advantage of another modern development—mar-proof plastic tops that look just like wood.

(1) To swing evenly, doors should have precisely aligned hinges. Look for magnetic catches (2) and glass set in behind narrow wooden strips (3).

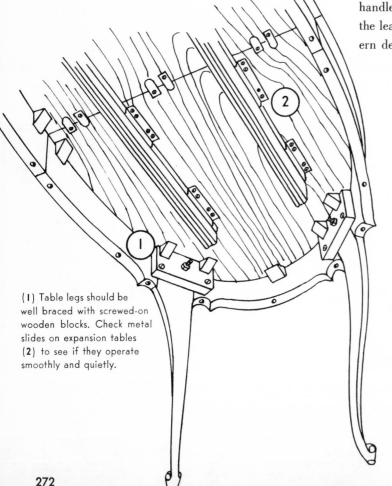

(1) Table legs should be well braced with screwed-on wooden blocks. Check metal slides on expansion tables (2) to see if they operate smoothly and quietly.

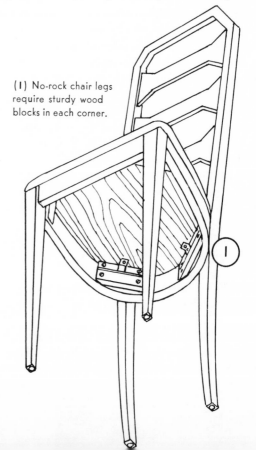

(1) No-rock chair legs require sturdy wood blocks in each corner.

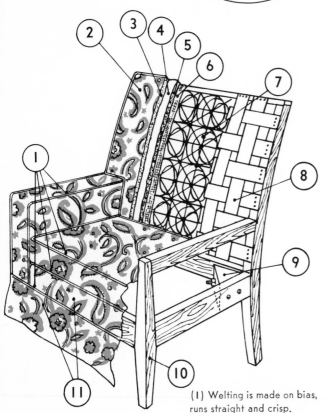

UPHOLSTERY

With upholstered furniture, quality becomes an inside story, told in the wood frame and layers of construction beneath the surface. Here you must base your selection largely on faith in the manufacturer's labels (happily, law requires him to be truthful about the contents). There are, however, certain signs of quality to watch out for, e.g., a sturdy frame of kiln-dried hardwood with tight-fitting doweled and glued joints and strong corner blocks. Beware of nails—they will work loose. Check the springs by feeling through the cambric dust cover on the bottom. In good furniture you will find either (1) handtied coil springs—at least eight, preferably 12, per seat—on a network of tightly meshed webbing, or (2) flat steel strips instead of webbing and flat S-type springs instead of coils. Filling material may be down (most luxurious and most expensive), curled cattletail hair, or a combination of horse and hog hair. The label must specify contents and the exact proportions of any mixture. Down and feathers are usually found in a 50-50 mixture; 15% horsehair with 85% hog hair is the acceptable ratio. Popular and very satisfactory fillers are polyurethane (or polyfoam) and latex foam rubber. The latter is usually found in medium- to higher-priced furniture. Avoid moss, tow and excelsior as they deteriorate quickly. Test for comfort by sitting on the piece. You should sink slowly without slipping from side to side. Bounce! The springs should never hit the frame. The outer covering depends on taste and needs. High price is no guarantee of durability. For family use, fabric with 100 per cent nylon surface and a tight nubby texture is a good choice. Also look for stain-repellent finishes, fabric matched at seams, welting cut on bias, fabric-covered decks under cushions, zippers in the cushion covers.

(1) Welting should be straight, cut on bias; look for self-covered deck (2), zippered cushions (3). Tufting (4) should be made by buttons actually sewn through filling. Cushions of layered latex foam, polyester fiber (5) outlive spring cushions. Doweled & glued joints (6).

(1) Welting is made on bias, runs straight and crisp. Peeled-back layers of upholstery, starting with surface fabric (2), include cotton batting (3) and muslin (4) to contain hair stuffing (5).

Next burlap (6) is stitched to springs (7). Under support comes from fabric webbing (8). Watch for wood blocks in corners (9), legs that are part of framework (10), matched fabric pattern (11).

PAINT: CANNED MAGIC

A paintbrush or roller is the nearest thing to a magic wand the home decorator can lay her hand on. Paint can perk up the plainest room, resuscitate tired furniture, cover a multitude of architectural sins. Priced by the yard, it's the most inexpensive and effective ally you can buy for the battle against drabness. There are hundreds of colors to choose from, dozens of finishes, a million magic tricks you can work all through your house. But before you start waving that magic brush about, brush up on your paint basics. Understanding what's available today, what each kind does best and how to use it will make painting almost as pleasant in the process as in the end.

First, almost all the countless cans of paint you'll see on your dealer's shelves have either a latex base or an alkyd base. The base, which is clearly stated on the can label, determines the character of the paint, so let's have a close look at each:

ALKYD-BASE PAINT

Thinned with solvents—e.g., turpentine. Available in flat, semigloss and gloss finishes for both inside and exterior use. Durable, water-resistant and therefore completely scrubbable. Brush strokes and lap marks will not show. Takes up to two hours to dry to the touch, overnight before pictures can be hung. Requires undercoat. Both odor and fumes present. Spills and tools must be cleaned with turpentine.

LATEX-BASE PAINT

Thinned with water. Available in flat finishes, flat enamels for interior and exterior use. Wash gently. Brush strokes and lap marks don't show. Dries so quickly pictures can be hung after an hour or so. May require special primer on some surfaces. Almost odorless. Soap and water are all you need for cleanup.

Other kinds of paint you may encounter include:

CEMENT PAINT

Special gloss paint that resists the alkali in concrete.

ENAMEL

Available in high, semigloss and low gloss which dry to a smooth, hard finish.

OIL-BASE PAINT

Comes in flat, semigloss and gloss. Thin with mineral spirits or paint thinner. Absorbs grease and is difficult to wash, so avoid using in bathroom or kitchen.

SEALER and PRIMER PAINT

Use to seal porous surface of raw wood or plaster before applying top coat of paint.

TEXTURE PAINT

Treated to create automatically surfaces with interesting textures—grain, flecks, crepe-like finishes. Comes in both cans and sprays.

UNDERCOAT

Use on nonporous surfaces to provide smooth surface for top coat.

VINYL PAINT

Completely washable, easy to use (water-thinned), dries quickly, covers well, has little odor.

For furniture, gloss or semigloss and enamel wear well. To antique furniture, try the new color glaze kits now widely available.

New tools have taken half the work out of painting. Aerosol spray cans cost a bit more but they are good to the last drop for such tricky surfaces as wicker and louvered shutters. You'll always need a few brushes for finishing touches, but investigate the new throwaway types, and the great variety of roller shapes and widths now available for every conceivable nook and cranny, and for painting wall designs.

FANTASTIC PLASTIC

It all started as a game a hundred or so years ago when an American scientist went looking for a substitute for ivory billiard balls. He came up with plastic, the versatile, durable material that has by now made itself very much at home in our homes. From the kitchen, where Formica was introduced during the 1920's, plastic has advanced through the house as technology has advanced its good looks and versatility. Now it's found underfoot, on the walls, and very much present—though not always accounted for—in furniture of all kinds. Plastic is rapidly replacing wood parts in furniture, both behind the scenes, where it's used for structural elements, drawer slides, etc., and on the surface, where decorative panels, "carved" legs, and such are actually plastic molded to look like wood. Plastic is so perfect in this role as *imitator* that even experts have to knock on "wood" to see if it's real.

But this is not to dismiss plastic as merely a substitute for the real thing. Often it actually does the job better. Certainly, it can do it more inexpensively in the case of ornate styles.

Plastic has another, totally modern role as *innovator,* where it plays itself. Plastic as *plastic*—molded into undulating chairs, chopped into block-like urethane-foam sofas, bent into crystal-clear acrylic tables, blown up into air- or styrene-bead-filled loveseats—is very uncliché, very Twenty-First Century.

Here's an introduction to plastics in the home:

ABS
Short for acrylonitrile-butadiene-styrene, combination of acrylic, polystyrene, rubber. Noted for resiliency, impact resistance. Found in chair, sofa frames, decorative elements.

ACRYLIC
Clear or colored, a favorite for chairs, cubes, tables. Resists moderate shocks, weather, most household chemicals (beware perfume, nail-care products, cleaning fluid). Scratches easily (cover with auto paste wax; anti-static spray reduces dust).

AMINO PLASTICS
Better known as MELAMINE and UREA in tableware, laminated table tops. Hard, scratch-resistant, impervious to household chemicals, but hard blows will shatter.

EPOXY
Found in synthetic marble table tops, decorative parts, trims. Durable, chemical-resistant.

NYLON
Used for drawer glides, bearings, wheels, etc. Extremely rugged, resistant to heat, abrasion, chemicals.

PHENOLICS
Molded into wood-particle-filled decorative panels. High heat and electrical resistance.

POLYESTER
Found in molded chairs, structural elements, decorative parts, ornamental table and counter tops. Resists weather, most chemicals.

POLYETHYLENE, PROPYLENE
Both from the olefin family. Used for molded modern furniture. Fairly durable.

POLYSTYRENE
Molded into decorative and structural parts—wood-grain legs, drum tables; shells for upholstered chairs. Suffers from severe impact, direct flame.

POLYURETHANE (or URETHANE)
Found as both rigid and flexible foam. Rigid foam used for shock- and abrasion-resistant chairs, sofa frames, decorative trim. Flexible foam found in seating cushions, modern furniture. Water, moisture, rot and vermin proof. The denser the foam, the better.

VINYL
In upholstery materials, veneers, laminates, coatings for wall-coverings, etc. Also inflatable furniture, chairs filled with tiny beads of expanded polystyrene. Don't come near with abrasive cleaners, nail-care products, moth repellents, direct heat.

WALLCOVERINGS: THE LOW-DOWN ON WHAT GOES UP

Walls are the most omnipresent element in any interior. Treat them offhandedly and they just stand around in the background. Treat them well and they'll more than carry their own weight in the decorative design of any room.

Modern wallcoverings have come a long way since the Chinese first rice-papered their walls about 200 B.C. Today, there are cloth and plastic "papers" you can scrub, put up easily yourself and remove just as easily merely by peeling. You can also cover walls with fabrics, with paneling in real wood, or products engineered to look like wood, stone, brick or even woven fabrics.

Carpeting is one of the newest materials to climb the walls, where it's a boon to soundproofing. Such soft wallcoverings are tufted just like floor carpeting, minus the heavy backing. They come in narrow widths and are applied with conventional adhesives.

Before you decide what kind of look you'd like for your walls, let's analyze today's wallcoverings:

WALLPAPER

Technically, you can no longer say "paper." The term lingers, like "ice box" for refrigerator, but today's wall*papers* are likely to be made from fabrics or plastics as well as paper. You'll find metallic finishes, plastic coatings, textured and flocked surfaces that look and feel like cut velvet. You'll also find a whole new look in those thick wallpaper books on your dealer's shelves. Far from the polite tints and timid patterns that filled your grandmother's house, there are super florals, great geometrics, snappy patterns that become an assertive part of your rooms' decor. Choose carefully and you can work real wonders with wallcoverings: Vertically striped paper will raise a low ceiling • Big, bold patterns will make a bare room look furnished • A wallpaper mural adds the illusion of openness to tight spaces • Used all over a room, including woodwork, doors, furniture and windows (there are many fabrics made to match), wallcoverings can unify broken-up space and cover architectural irregularities. Other wallpaper terms to help guide you in your selection:

FLOCKS

Powdered wool or synthetic fibers adhered to backing in textile-like patterns that look and feel like velvet, but can often be washed with soap and water.

GRASSCLOTH

Originally handmade in Japan by gluing native grasses onto paper, it also means wallcoverings printed or textured to look like the real thing.

HAND-BLOCKED

Paper printed via individually engraved wooden blocks. Expensive because of the time and labor involved.

LINER PAPER

Used when walls are so rough irregularities would show through the new wallcovering.

PLASTICS

Found in supple, easy-to-hang wallcoverings, and as protective coatings to make papers washable and stain-resistant.

PRE-PASTED

Paper with paste already applied. The do-it-yourselfer has only to draw it through a water box to activate glue.

PRE-TRIMMED

Wallpaper with the selvages removed at the factory for easy application.

ROLL

Or bolt, of paper, containing 36 square feet (count on 30 usable square feet). Most paper comes in double or triple rolls, but prices are quoted by the single roll.

SILK-SCREENING

Or hand-screening. Wallpaper printed by forcing paint through a design applied to a silk-covered screen. Less expensive than hand-blocked paper, but more than paper printed by machine, as the vast majority is.

STRIPPABLE

Relatively new and splendid development in wallcoverings, strippable papers are chemically treated so they can be pulled off the wall, strip by strip, without marring it. Often no water is required.

VINYL

Plastic found frequently in wallcoverings, as a coating to allow easy washing, or laminated to a paper or fabric backing.

PANELING

Wood has warmed our rooms and hearts so long it tends to be synonymous with the word "paneling." But there's a lot more in today's decorating vocabulary. Paneling can look like leather, like tile, like tapestries. It can be given interesting geometric textures and molded of lightweight fiber glass or plastic to look so much like stone or brick you'd have to touch to be sure. No matter what form it takes, most paneling comes in standard sizes (generally 4 x 8 feet) and can be applied by any reasonably handy man.

For unusual effects, there are panels of grillwork. And don't overlook the possibility of achieving the impact of expensive carved paneling with carved doors grouped together across the wall or horizontally as wainscoting.

In general, you will find three categories of paneling: solid wood, plywood and hardboard:

SOLID WOOD

Elegant, heavy and costly. Application usually left to professionals because it's difficult to handle.

PLYWOOD

Real wood in every sense, but engineered for strength, stability and surface beauty. Consists of at least three plies of wood bonded together under a surface veneer of real wood (or, sometimes, wood-grained vinyl). Almost any kind of wood can be found, from plain knotty pine to the exotics, plus some familiar woods given unusual surface finishes. Many plywood panels also have protective surface finishes to increase their durability and cleanability.

HARDBOARDS

Also an engineered wood product, discovered in 1924. Wood fibers are pressed into dense boards that can be sawed and hammered just like any wood. Can be finished to look like any wood, too, down to the dimensional grains. Or may simulate tiles, fabrics, leather, patterned wallpaper, etc. Generally less expensive than plywood.

LIGHTING: THE BRIGHTEST IDEAS IN DECORATING

Fashion has finally turned the spotlight on home lighting. Lamps look like works of art; tables and bookcases come with built-in illumination; pedestals light up their own sculptures. New materials, especially the plastics, have led us from the Dark Ages to this bright new era in which designers can bend, mold and shape lamps and lighting fixtures into truly 20th-century designs. Until the 1960's or so, home lighting had simply followed the traditional forms of candlelight, using electricity instead of fire. We now have a whole new vocabulary of expressions in home lighting. Don't be content to talk in the old terms of ceiling-fixture-plus-lamps until you've seen how exciting today's lighting can be, and what it can do for your rooms.

Along with modern lamps and illuminated furniture, you will find more traditional—but less-often employed—forms of lighting, such as recessed spotlights in the ceiling; coves, cornices and valances; illuminated walls and ceilings that shed their glow over the entire room. Many such fixtures come prepackaged with the do-it-yourselfer in mind, considerably cutting the cost of built-in lighting.

This new emphasis is long overdue. Lighting has always been the most overlooked aspect of home decorating, despite the fact that it affects everything else in the room. It can change colors radically (see the chapter on color selection). It can make a vast room feel cozy, divide free-flowing floor plans into distinct areas and create instant atmosphere for gracious dining and entertaining. Good lighting makes a room inviting. People are attracted to it like moths. Poor lighting can be depressing, both physically and psychologically, while over-bright lighting can cause eye-strain and brittle tempers.

To make the most of lighting's possibilities, understand all its aspects, beginning at its very source with the assortment of bulbs readily available today.

BULBS

have changed importantly since Edison's original version made of clear glass with a bent bamboo filament. Incandescent bulbs now come in a variety of whites and soft colors, with coatings to diffuse the light gently and different wattages to suit different needs. Fluorescent bulbs, once coldly office-like, have also been softened for home use. In general, they still give a whiter, bluer light than incandescent bulbs, which tend toward a yellowish glow. And, in general, fluorescent lights last longer and generate less heat. Both sources can have drastic effects on colors in a room.

Basically, all lighting falls into two categories, general and specific.

GENERAL LIGHTING

is overall illumination that lets you carry on most of your activities. Think of it as the equivalent of daylight, since, like the sun, it usually comes from overhead. Ceiling fixtures, valances, coves or diffused recessed spotlights all contribute to general lighting.

SPECIFIC LIGHTING

focuses on a specific area, for a specific purpose. Pinpoint ceiling spots, hanging lights over a bedside table, a chandelier over a dining table all fall in this category. However, lamps are by far the most popular form of specific lighting, and the easiest to buy, once you understand the guidelines for good lamp-lighting.

LAMPS

should be proportionate to the table on which they will sit, tall enough so you don't look down on the bright bulb when you stand, low enough so you don't look up into it when you sit. Allow 38 to 42 inches from shade bottom to the floor for table lamps; 47 to 49 inches for floor lamps.

Keep the shapes of bases and shades simple. Lamps are accessories, not center pieces. Candlesticks, urns, vases and some of the streamlined modern shapes are always in good taste for bases. Traditional shades come in four basic types:

Drum shades are deep, with the top about an inch wider than the bottom.
Pancake shades are fairly shallow with straight sides.
Bouillotte shades (named for the 18th-century card game they lighted) are very shallow with slanted sides.
Empire shades have sharply slanting sides, with the bottom about twice as wide as the top.

For proper proportion, a shade should be two-thirds as tall as the base. For proper lighting, it should be either translucent, to diffuse the light, or opaque with a white lining to direct it sharply up and down. Never, never choose a shade that allows the bulb to glare through its sides. Watch this tendency in some contemporary globe lights. Always see a lamp lighted in the showroom, away from other lamps, before you buy.

CHANDELIERS

the other most popular form of specific lighting, are also decorative as well as practical. And neither function should be neglected when you choose them. Again, think proportion: too large and a chandelier will hover oppressively over a small room. Too small and it will look lost against an ocean of ceiling space, rendering its light altogether useless. Too bright and it will be annoying. Keep bulbs small—seldom above 25 watts—and well shaded unless you use tiny candle lights. And always hang chandeliers above eye level, between 30 and 36 inches above a dining room table.

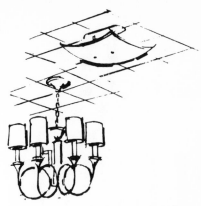

CEILING FIXTURES, including chandeliers and hanging lamps, are prime sources of general lighting.

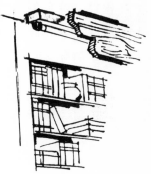

A CORNICE attached to the ceiling over bookshelves, etc., adds the illusion of height to the room.

VALANCE STRIPS are mounted over draperies and left open on top to reflect light both up and down.

CEILINGS and walls can be illuminated from behind translucent panels for dramatic lighting effects.

VII GLOSSARY OF HOME FURNISHINGS

A

A-FRAME

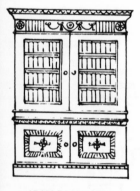

ADAM BOOKCASE

ADAM BENCH

ABS—Mercifully shortened identification for acrylonitrile-butadiene-styrene plastics, extremely durable material often found molded into home furnishings.

A-FRAME—Simple house design based on triangle or "A" shape with sharply sloping roof. Relatively inexpensive; popular in vacation areas.

ACCENT—A small item or amount of something that gives a room lots of decorating punch—e.g., a brightly contrasting color used in small doses.

ACCESSORIES—The small elements in a room that add personality, individuality, a lived-in look—lamps, pillows, pictures, plants, etc.

ACETATE (and triacetate)—Generic name for a man-made fiber first introduced in 1924 and now found under a variety of trade names. Has pleasing hand, good draping and sun-resistant qualities.

ACRYLIC (a-*cryl*-ik) (and modacrylic)—A man-made chemical fiber discovered about 1950; found under various trade names in long-lived fabrics and carpets. In the latter, they look, feel and wear much like wool. You'll also find see-through and colored acrylics molded into modern furniture.

ADAM—The Brothers Adam, Robert and James, were late 18th-century English architects who came home from studies in Italy to lead the return to classicism in houses and furnishings. Among their eager followers: Chippendale, Hepplewhite and Sheraton.

APRON

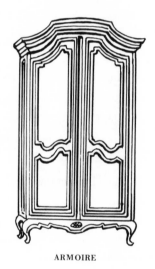

ARMOIRE

ART NOUVEAU TABLE

A.I.D.—American Institute of Interior Designers, a professional organization for designers founded in 1930. Headquarters: 730 Fifth Avenue, New York City, 10019.

ALKYD (*al*-kid)—Durable, washable paint; thin with mineral spirits.

ANTIQUE—Officially, according to U.S. Customs law, anything more than 100 years old. Generally, anything from a specific period in history is called "antique"—e.g., late Victorian.

ANTIQUED—Furniture painted and finished to achieve the worn, mellow look that comes with age.

ANTIQUE SATIN—See Satin.

APRON—On windows, the horizontal finishing strip of wood beneath the sill. On furniture, the horizontal boxing strip under a table top.

AREA RUG—Small rug which, as its name implies, is used to set off a special area.

ARMOIRE (arm-*wahr*)—Tall, usually heavy cabinet with two doors. Born in France for the storage of tools, now back on the contemporary scene holding everything from the television to clothes and curios.

ART DECO (ar-*deh*-ko)—Design form from the twenties, revitalized in the seventies; features flat geometric prints in slightly off-key colors.

ART NOUVEAU (ar-noo-*vo*)—"New Art," literally, when it emerged around 1900 with sensuous, swirling lines borrowed from plant tendrils. Enjoyed a renaissance in the late 1960s.

ASPHALT TILE—Least expensive

of the resilient floorings but also the least versatile.

AUBUSSON (oh-bu-*son*) —The light-colored, tapestry-like carpets woven at Aubusson, France, beginning during the reign of Louis XIV and still being produced.

AUSTRIAN SHADE—Elegant, formal window treatment made by gathering sheer fabric into swags across the window. Can be raised and lowered.

AWNING WINDOW—Window with horizontal sections that open simultaneously.

AXMINSTER—Kind of loom first used in Axminster, England, to weave tufted carpets with soft pile, stiff jute backing; hence, carpets woven on such a loom.

B

BACKING—Sturdy material (jute, polypropylene or olefin) into which carpet yarns are tufted; often coated with latex to bind the yarns then, in better quality carpets, topped with another layer of backing ("double backing").

BAIL—Hoop-shaped metal pull on furniture, often attached to decorative back-plate.

BALL-AND-CLAW (or claw-and-ball) FOOT—Chinese motif of a dragon's claw clutching a pearl, adopted by European furniture makers and adapted into an eagle's claw by 18th-century American designers.

BALL FRINGE—Bouncy, informal fringe with fluffy pompons hanging from woven heading.

BANQUETTE (*ban*-ket) — Seating arrangements built in along wall, usually for dining.

BARCELONA CHAIR—Now-classic leather chair on X-shaped steel supports designed by architect Mies Van

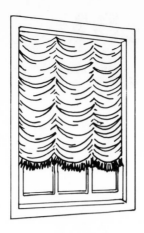

AUSTRIAN SHADE

BAIL

BALL-AND-CLAW

BARCELONA CHAIR

der Rohe and first exhibited in Barcelona, Spain, in 1929.

BAROQUE (bah-*rhok*) — Swirling, over-sized and over-elegant style of ornamentation that flourished in 16th-century Italy and spread all over Europe.

BASKET WEAVE—Loosely woven fabric such as hopsacking or oxford cloth.

BAUHAUS (bough-house) — Famous German school of design founded in 1919 by Walter Gropius; it is still influential today, although it was destroyed in World War II.

BAY WINDOW—Group of windows forming an angled projection from a room.

BELTER — John, mid-19th-century cabinet maker whose New York shop turned out elaborately curved and carved furniture in the best Victorian manner.

BENTWOOD—As its name implies, wood bent and shaped under steam and pressure into rather elegant, streamlined designs. Process was developed in the 19th century and put to good use by Michael Thonet, an Austrian furniture designer who is best known for his chairs.

BERGERE (bear-jhair)—Wide, wood-framed upholstered armchair. The French word actually means shepherdess, whose wide skirts such chairs accommodated gracefully.

BESTPLEAT—Ready-made tape for drapery headings; pinches automatically into pleats when companion hooks are inserted.

BIEDERMEIER (bee-der-mi-er) — Heavy, plump and slightly pompous style of furniture from 19th-century Austria, named after a philistine comic character in a Viennese newspaper.

BLEND—Two or more fibers mixed to produce fabric with special properties.

BLOCK FRONT—Desks, chests, secretaries, etc., with fronts made of

BENTWOOD

BERGERE

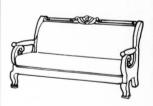

BIEDERMEIER SOFA

BLOCK FRONT

BOMBE

thick boards that are cut in a series of three curves—convex, concave, convex. Most often found on American pieces and attributed to cabinet maker John Goddard of Newport, Rhode Island.

BOLSTER—Round or triangular cushion used for back or arm rest.

BOMBE (bom-*bay*)—French, meaning "blown out"; usually applied to chests which bulge out in center front with smaller swells at the sides.

BONDED—Fabric adhered to fabric or to foam for improved strength and appearance.

BORAX—Furniture industry slang for homely, over-elaborate furniture. Derives from coupons once carried by cleaning product entitling purchaser to obtain furniture.

BOUCLE (boo-*clay*)—Fabric with surface loops; from the French word for "ringed."

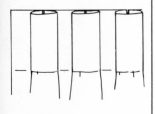

BOX PLEATS

BOULLE (bool)—Type of elaborate marquetry, usually in tortoise shell and brass, developed by Andre Charles Boulle and favored by Louis XIV. Often the delicate inlays are protected by gilt metal mounts.

BOW WINDOW—Window that curves outward from room.

BOX PLEATS—Neat, precise pleats made by sewing flat folds at spaced intervals across the top of draperies, slipcover skirts, dust ruffles, etc.

BRACKET FOOT

BRACKET FOOT—Simple, squarish foot formed from two pieces of wood angled together at the corner.

BRAID—Flat, decorative tape with edges finished alike.

BREAKFRONT—Large, tall storage unit with lower cabinet topped by shelves, often enclosed with glass.

BROADLOOM—Carpet woven on a broad loom. Today's advertisements might indicate otherwise, but it is not a standard of quality or style.

BROCADE—Elegant fabric with all-over raised design of figures or flowers woven in.

BREAKFRONT

BROKEN PEDIMENT

BULL'S EYE

BUTTERFLY TABLE

CABRIOLE LEG

BROCATELLE (brock-a-*tel*)—Flat fabric woven with two different size yarns; has a puffed effect on surface. Good for upholstery.

BROKEN PEDIMENT—When the pediment, or arch, above a door or atop case furniture, mirrors, etc., is interrupted and the space filled with a decorative element.

BRUSSELS CARPET—Carpet with a looped woolen pile and cotton back.

BUCKRAM—Fabric with stiff finish used for interlinings.

BULLION—Trimming with heavy, tightly twisted fringe; used for epaulets and decoration.

BULL'S EYE—Small round mirror with convex or concave glass and an ornate gilt frame; fashionable in the early 19th century.

BUREAU—A chest of drawers, often with matching mirror. The English, however, mean a writing desk with drawers when they say "bureau."

BUREAU-PLAT (bu-row pla)—The French agree with the English (above), meaning a flat writing table on tall legs with drawers just under the top. Became popular in late 17th-century France.

BURL—An anomaly in the tree (a knot or growth) which produces beautifully patterned grains when sliced into veneers.

BURLAP—Coarse, heavy-grained fabric made from jute, hemp or cotton.

BUTTERFLY TABLE — Drop-leaf table with wing-like supports that swing out to hold up the leaves.

C

CABRIOLE LEG (cab-ree-*ole*) — Gracefully curving leg with rounded knee, which takes its name from a French dancing term and took the fancy of 18th-century furniture makers in England and America.

CAFE CURTAIN—Cheerful little curtain borrowed from French coffee houses; rings and rod usually exposed.

CALICO—Calcutta, India, gave us this very old and still very popular, plain-weave fabric.

CAMELBACK—Chair or sofa with a curved hump in back; a Hepplewhite favorite.

CAMPAIGN FURNITURE—Handsome by-product of Napoleon's marches, it was designed so his officers could take some of the comforts of home along on campaigns. Chests stack, chairs fold, corners are often edged with brass, handles abound.

CANAPE (can-ah-pay)—French word for sofa.

CANDLE STAND—Three-legged, often elaborated turned and carved stand for candlesticks, candelabrum or lamp. Also known as a gueridon or torchere, although the latter now means a floor lamp that casts its light up.

CANDLEWICK—Muslin worked with heavy yarn loops which are cut and fluffed to imitate chenille; a bedspread favorite.

CANE—Flexible rattan woven for chair seats and backs, cabinet doors, etc. Another Oriental idea that found Occidental popularity.

CANOPY—Suspended drapery, usually over a bed. Once upon a time it served to close out the "dangerous" night airs; now it's highly decorative.

CAPTAIN'S CHAIR—Wood chair with low, rounded back, wide arms and turned legs.

CAROLEAN (kair-ah-lee-an)—The period when Charles I and II ruled England (1625-85). Furniture showed both French and Flemish influences. Look for spiral turnings, S- and C-curves, walnut, which rivaled oak in popularity.

CARTOUCHE (kar-toosh)—Fanciful unrolled scroll motif often found on Philadelphia Chippendale highboys, clocks and mirrors.

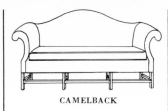
CAMELBACK

CAMPAIGN FURNITURE

CAPTAIN'S CHAIR

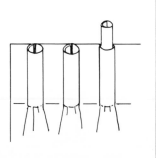
CARTRIDGE PLEATS

CARTRIDGE PLEATS—Round drapery pleats stuffed with crinoline to hold their shape.

CARYATID (kary-ah-tid)—Upright support carved in the shape of a human, usually a woman. The women of Carya supposedly started it all when they betrayed the Greeks to the Persians and were thus immured as punishment.

CASE GOODS—Wood furniture (chests, buffets, etc.) as opposed to upholstered furniture.

CASEIN (ka-seen)—Milk-protein material used in water-based paints.

CASSONE (kas-so-nee)—A dower chest originally designed to hold the Italian bride's linens. Very popular in the 15th and 16th centuries when it was lavishly decorated.

CASTERS—Small, swiveling rollers that make it easy to move furniture.

CATHEDRAL CEILING—Dramatic sloping ceiling more than one-story tall. Often found in contemporary houses.

CAUCASIAN RUGS—See Oriental rugs.

CHAINETTE FRINGE—Silky fringe made of yarn resembling a chain; a favorite for Austrian shades.

CHAISE-LONGUE—French for elongated lounging chair; sometimes comes with ottoman.

CHAMFER—Beveled or canted edge.

CHASED—Metal surface ornamented by engraving, embossing, etching, etc.

CHENILLE—Yarn with such fuzzy pile it looks like a caterpillar ("chenille" in French). Found in tassels, rugs, draperies, bedspreads.

CHEST-ON-CHEST—Chest of drawers in two sections.

CRETONNE (cree-ton)—Chintz-like drapery and slipcover fabric of cotton, linen or rayon. Developed in France by a Monsieur Cretonne.

CARYATID

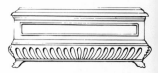
CASSONE

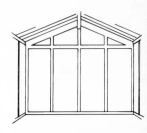
CATHEDRAL CEILING

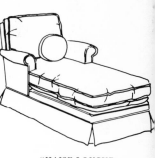
CHAISE-LONGUE

CHEST-ON-CHEST

CHEVAL-GLASS

CHEVRON

CHIPPENDALE

CLUB CHAIR

CHEVAL-GLASS—Large mirror mounted in a frame so it swings.

CHEVRON—V-shaped decoration.

CHIFFONIER (chif-fon-*neer*)—Both a tall chest of drawers (French) and a low cupboard with shelves for books (English) go by this name.

CHINOISERIE (shin-*wahz*-o-ree)—Decoration in the Chinese manner, particularly as done by China-admirers in 18th-century England and Italy.

CHINTZ—Glazed cotton fabric, often with large flower designs. Takes its name from the Hindu word for "spotted."

CHIPPENDALE—The man, Thomas, was a London cabinetmaker, who, in 1754 published the book of English furniture designs that turned his name into a famous style. Characterized by flowing lines, lavish carvings, a hint of Gothic and Chinese influence. Wildly popular in America, especially among Philadelphia cabinet makers.

CITY MIX—Furnishings of assorted styles blended to produce the kind of sophisticated room popular in the big cities. See Eclectic.

CLASSICAL—Traditionally designed, especially in the manner of ancient Greece and Rome.

CLERESTORY (*kleer*-story)—Narrow, long window that runs below the roof line to light a room from above.

CLUB CHAIR—Comfortable, well upholstered easy chair.

COFFEE (or cocktail) TABLE—Most American addition to home furnishings since the rocking chair, these are low tables (or substitutes) used in front of the sofa for the service of beverages, etc.

COGSWELL CHAIR—Has open arms with small upholstered sections.

COLONIAL—American furnishings from 1700 to 1781, after we'd conquered the wilderness and could relax into the niceties of life. Also known as American Georgian, it's the era Colonial Williamsburg personifies.

COMMODE

CONSOLE

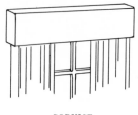

CORNICE

DANTE CHAIR

COLORFAST—Describes fabrics guaranteed not to fade under normal use.

COMMODE—French word for small, low chest used against a wall.

COMPLEMENTARY — Decorating scheme based on colors that lie directly opposite each other on the color wheel (e.g., red and green).

CONSOLE—Table used against a wall; usually supported by legs or brackets in front only.

CONTEMPORARY—Now! Furnishings designed and made today, of today's materials. Often a synonym for Modern, although Modern generally means the kind of form-follows-function design that began with the Bauhaus.

CORNICE—Decorative strip of wood, drapery or fabric-covered buckram concealing drapery headings, or bulbs for indirect lighting.

COVE—Concave molding at ceiling line; often used to conceal fixtures for indirect lighting.

CREDENZA — Italian sideboard or buffet.

CUBE—Neat little boxes in a variety of materials found on today's decorating scene serving as small tables, sculpture supports, etc.

CURTAIN—Window hanging, generally lighter weight than draperies.

CUSHIONED VINYL — Comfortable, sound-absorbing resilient floor covering made by laminating sheet vinyl to a foam-cushion base.

CUT VELVET—Velvet with sculptured designed.

D

DADO (*day*-do)—When lower part of wall is decorated differently from top, it is called a dado.

DAMASK—Firm, glossy fabric with flat design. Ever since Marco Polo opened the fabric trade between Damascus and the Western World, it has been a favorite for tablecloths, napkins, draperies, upholstery.

DANTE (*don*-tay) **CHAIR**—Heavy, X-shaped chair that dates back to 16th-century Italy.

DIMITY (*dim*-it-ee) — Thin, sheer cotton, often with woven-in cords or stripes; easy to work, launders well. Often used for bedspreads.

DIRECTOIRE (deer-reck-*twar*)— Period following the French Revolution (1792-1804) characterized by classical motifs, simple, graceful furniture that made the transition from the Neoclassicism of Louis XVI to Napoleon's Empire style.

DIRECTOR'S CHAIR — Wood or metal armchair with canvas sling seat and back that folds flat, scissors-style. Hollywood made it a star.

DIRECTORY—Period when the French Directoire influence rubbed off on America (1805-25), producing a master of the style in Duncan Phyfe.

DISC FOOT—Flat, round foot often found on Queen Anne pieces.

DISTRESSED — Furniture scarred and painted to look aged.

DOCUMENTARY—Wallpaper, fabric, etc., printed with historical design —such as a Civil War motif.

DORMER—Window set in a gable or projecting from sloping roof.

DOUBLE-HUNG WINDOW— Standard window with two moveable sashes.

DOUBLE-WOVEN — Two different fabrics woven simultaneously and joined by binder threads. Drapery and lining materials may be double-woven.

DOVETAIL—Joint used in furniture making where dovetail-shaped projections on one piece fit into matching slots on another. Found in good quality drawers.

DIRECTOR'S CHAIR

DISC FOOT

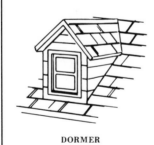

DORMER

DOVETAIL

DOWEL—Headless pin, usually of wood, used in furniture construction.

DOWN—Small fluffy under-feathers of fowl used to fill cushions in expensive upholstered furniture.

DRAPERY—Heavy fabric (when compared to curtains) which covers windows. Never "drapes."

DRESSER—Chest of drawers with mirror.

DROP FRONT (or drop lid) — Hinged desk front that falls forward to provide writing surface.

DROP HANDLE—Pendant handle, usually of brass. Also called tear drop and pear drop.

DROP LEAF — Table with hinged leaves that can be raised to extend top area.

DRUM TABLE — Round table on pedestal base with deep apron, often with drawers.

DRY SINK—"Dry" because the water had to be brought in for this Early American cupboard and poured into the zinc or copper-lined well in the top. Has two doors below for storage. Today they are much sought for use as bars and planters.

DUCK FOOT—Three-toed foot style that does indeed resemble a duck's foot. Also called drake or web foot.

DUTCH CUPBOARD—Large buffet topped with open shelves to show off china.

E

EAMES, CHARLES (eems)—20th-century designer best known for his now-classic contour lounge chairs of molded plywood and leather.

EARLY AMERICAN—The furniture and unsophisticated surroundings of the first settlers in the New World (1608-1720), who were too busy stay-

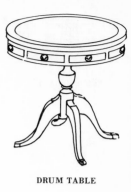

DRUM TABLE

DRY SINK

DUCK FOOT

EAMES CHAIR

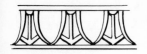

EGG AND DART

ELIZABETHAN CHAIR

ESCUTCHEON

ETAGERE

ing alive to think much about refinements. Furniture is provincial version of English 17th-century styles, made in maple or pine.

ECLECTIC (ek-*lek*-tik)—A mixture of furnishings from different periods and places carefully chosen to produce an interesting blend.

EGG-AND-DART — Popular design motif, traceable to the Greeks, featuring alternating egg-like and dart-like forms.

ELIZABETHAN—Strictly speaking, furniture made during reign of Elizabeth I (1558-1603), but actually showing influences from preceding Tudor and following Jacobean periods. Furniture was massive, squarish, with Gothic motifs, heavy carving, bulbous legs.

EMBOSSING—Fabric treated with heated rollers to produce a raised design on the surface.

EMPIRE—Napoleon's style: heavy, masculine, ornamented with his "N" and military symbols. Egyptian and Roman motifs popular.

ENAMEL — Hard, satiny furniture finish, usually in a vivid color, produced on wood by buffing, on metal by baking.

ENGLISH REGENCY — England's version (1780-1820) of the neoclassicism that was sweeping the design world, later producing the Empire period in France and Federal period in America. English Regency furniture was smallish and graceful, decorated with sphinxes, Greek-key borders and other classical motifs.

ESCUTCHEON (es-*kutch*-un)—Protective metal ornament used around keyhole or as back plate for handle.

ETAGERE (ay-ta-*jehr*) — French word for open shelves, either free-standing or hanging. They are a handsome way to show off a collection of books, bibelots, etc.

EXPANDED VINYL — Plastic upholstery fabric chemically treated so it expands and becomes thicker, glove-like.

FAUTEUIL

FERRULE

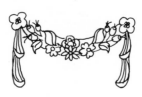

FESTOON

FIDDLE BACK

F

FABRIC FINISH — Special treatment applied to fabrics (under a variety of trade names) to make them soil-and-stain resistant.

FAIENCE (fay-*ahnz*) — Tin-glazed earthenware. The term comes from Faenza, Italy, but was adopted for ceramics produced in France.

FAILLE (file)—Silk or rayon fabric with crosswise rib effect. Used for draperies.

FAUTEUIL (fo-*too*-ee)—French word for armchair. Upholstered, but with open arms as opposed to the bergere.

FEDERAL STYLE—Elegant, classic furniture that flourished in America after the Revolution (about 1781-1830). Influenced by England (Hepplewhite, Sheraton) and France (Directoire and Empire). Look for the spread eagle, Stars and Stripes, red-white-and-blue color schemes, other symbols of America's emerging identity.

FELT — A matted, compact mostly woolen cloth which requires no hemming.

FERRULE (*fair*-rul)—Metal band or cap at the base of wood leg.

FESTOON—Carved or painted ornamentation showing garlands or ropes in decorative loops; also decorative scallops of cord added to draperies, bedspreads, etc., and accented with tassels.

FIBERS, SYNTHETIC — See Synthetic Fibers.

FIBREGLAS—See Glass Fibers.

FIDDLE BACK—Chair with violin shaped splat back.

FILIGREE — Lacy, delicate metal ornament on furniture.

FILLING — The stuffing in upholstered furniture which may be natural hair or man-made material such as polyurethane (polyfoam).

FINIAL—Decorative ornament on top of bedpost, lamp, etc.

FIRE-SCREEN — Free-standing screens, often in needlework, used as protection from the fierce heat and flying sparks of yesteryear's large fireplaces. Now charming accessories in period rooms.

FLAME STITCH—Undulating, multi-colored pattern adapted from traditional Hungarian needlework stitch.

FLAT FABRIC—Any fabric woven of equal size yarns to produce a smooth finish.

FLOCK—Powdered wool or synthetic applied to fabric or wallpaper to give three-dimensional elegance. Flocked carpet has sculptured surface created by electrostatically adhering nylon pile fibers to a foundation layer.

FLOKATI—Delightfully shaggy wool carpets woven by Greek peasants.

FLUORESCENT LIGHTS — Elongated bulbs coated inside with fluorite, which glows when exposed to electrons.

FLUTING—Narrow vertical grooves borrowed from classic architecture and often used as a decorative motif on furniture.

FRAME—Skeleton inside upholstered furniture. Occasionally left exposed, as in many Scandinavian pieces.

FREE-STANDING — Furniture not dependent on wall for support, either physically or visually, e.g., a sofa is said to be free-standing when it is used in the center of the room.

FRENCH PROVINCIAL — Charming country cousin of the elegant 17th- and 18th-century French court furniture, as translated by craftsmen in the provinces. Look for painted finishes, checked fabrics, toile de Jouy patterns, straw chair seats, and abundant accessories.

FRETWORK—Lattice work, usually in geometric designs; a motif borrowed from the Chinese.

FINIAL

FIRE-SCREEN

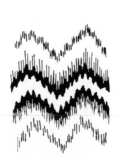

FLAME STITCH

G

GADROON (gad-*droon*)—Decorative band of raised oval shapes; often found on silver or tabletops.

GALLERY—Miniature railing on top of cabinet or table.

GALLOON (ga-*loon*)—Flat, closely woven braid used for upholstery and trimming draperies. Like gimp, but wider.

GATE-LEG TABLE—Drop-leaf table with legs that swing, gate-like, to support the leaves.

GEORGIAN—Period during the reign of all four Georges of England (1715-1830), when Chippendale, Sheraton, the Adam Brothers and Hepplewhite were making design history. Prosperous colonists commissioned local craftsmen to copy the styles, thus producing American Georgian—see Colonial.

GESSO (*jes*-so) — Ornamentations molded or carved from plaster and painted or gilded.

GILT—Thin layer of gold or gold-colored material washed over an article.

GIMP—Narrow ornamental trimming (about ½-inch wide) developed for use on upholstery, now popular in other decorative roles.

GINGHAM—Lightweight cotton fabric, usually woven in checks or stripes.

GIRONDOLE (*jir*-ahn-dole) — Mirror, usually convex, with candle sconces attached.

GLASS CURTAIN — Sheer window covering that does, in fact, hang next to the glass. Often used under heavier draperies.

GLASS FIBERS — Fibers manufactured from glass and made into soft, wrinkleless, fire-resistant fabrics with good draping qualities. Can also be bonded with plastic and molded into everything from chairs to automobile

FLUTING

GADROON

GATE-LEG TABLE

GIRONDOLE

287

GOTHIC

GUERIDON

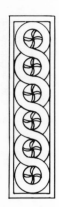

GUILLOCHE

HADLEY CHEST

bodies. Fiberglas is the trademark of glass fiber products from its major developer, Owens-Corning Fiberglas Corp.

GOBELINS (go-*blan*) — France's famous state-supported center of the decorative arts, established in 1667 under the direction of Charles Le Brun. Perhaps best known for its tapestries.

GOTHIC—13th-century architecture style revisited by mid-19th-century furniture makers, who borrowed its pointed arches and trefoil motifs.

GRILLE—Metal latticework, usually brass, often backed with fabric, used as cabinet paneling.

GROS POINT—Coarse embroidery used in upholstery. From the French meaning "large needle," as opposed to petit point, or "small needle."

GUERIDON (gay-ree-*doe*)—Small, round French table used as a candlestand.

GUILLOCHE (gil-*lowsh*)—Ornamental band of intertwining figure 8's or ribbons enclosing a circular motif.

H

HADLEY CHEST—Early American chest, ornately carved, found mainly in the neighborhood of Hadley, Mass.

HARDBOARD — Engineered wood product of wood fibers compressed into dense boards, then finished to look like wood, marble, leather, etc. Tough, inexpensive paneling material.

HARDWOOD—Wood from leaf-bearing trees, as opposed to wood from evergreens, which is softer, e.g., pine.

HARVEST TABLE—Long, narrow table with straight legs, drop-leaf sides; originally used in farmhouse kitchens.

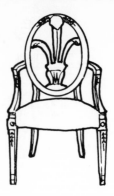

HEPPLEWHITE CHAIR

HITCHCOCK CHAIR

HOOP BACK

INVERTED CUP LEGS

HASSOCK—Fully upholstered footstool.

HAUT RELIEF (*oh*-relief)—French for high relief or greatly raised surface decoration, as opposed to bas (low) relief.

HEADING—Treatment at the top of draperies.

HEPPLEWHITE—Dignified and refined furniture style developed by George Hepplewhite, London cabinet maker who worked in the mid-to-late 18th century. Look for square legs, satinwood, shield or oval chair backs.

HIGHBOY—Tall chest of drawers mounted on a long-legged commode or lowboy. America's unique contribution to furniture design.

HITCHCOCK CHAIR—Painted and stenciled wood chair made famous by Lambert Hitchcock of Connecticut, who mass-produced them in the first half of the 19th century.

HOMESPUN—Slightly coarse, irregular fabrics machine-loomed to look handmade. Popular for informal decoration.

HOOP BACK—Chair with top rail bent into half-hoop, as found on one type of Windsor chair.

HUE—Synonym for color; e.g., red is a hue.

HUTCH — Open storage unit with shelves, usually used atop a buffet.

I

INCISED — Decoration deeply engraved or carved into the surface.

INLAY—Decoration formed by insetting contrasting material — ivory, wood, shell, etc.—into incised surface.

INTAGLIO (in-*tal*-yo)—Italian for carved design sunk below the surface.

288

ITALIAN PROVINCIAL — Simplified version of French and Italian Directoire style furniture popularly —and erroneously—thought to have originated in the Italian provinces.

INTENSITY — The strength of a color; e.g., the difference between pink and fire engine red is a matter of intensity.

INVERTED CUP — Chair or table-leg turnings that resemble an upside-down cup.

J

JABOT

JABOT (zha-*bow*) — Folded drapery cut diagonally across bottom and used at side of swag window treatment.

JACOBEAN (jack-oh-*bee*-an) — Heavy oak furniture, often with bulbous or twisted legs, made during the reign of James I of England (1603-25) and later. Jacobus is the Latinized form of James.

JACOBEAN CHAIR

JACQUARD (*jack*-kard — Intricate method of weaving invented in early 19th century by J. J. M. Jacquard and still used for such fabrics as brocade and damask.

JALOUSIE (zha-lu-see) — Window with many overlapping horizontal sections that open and close, a kind of built-in venetian blind of glass.

KAS

JAPANNING (ja-*panning*) — The Western world's attempts to copy the East's painstaking method of building up layers of varnish. In japanning, paint is often substituted for varnish.

JARDINIERE (zhar-din-*air*) — Container for plants; from the French word for garden.

JASPE (zhas-*pay*) — Drapery and upholstery fabric with faint, woven-in stripes of three variations of one color.

JUTE — Tough, heavy vegetable fiber from India often used for carpet backing.

KETTLE FRONT

K

KAS — Large cupboards, Dutch or Pennsylvania Dutch, with paintings or carving.

KETTLE FRONT — Case piece with bulging front, usually 18th century.

KLISMOS (klis-mos) — The Greeks' elegantly simple chair, armless with curving back and legs. Much illustrated on classic urns and often borrowed for modern designs.

KNEEHOLE DESK — Desk with center hole to accommodate the knees of person working there.

KNIFE EDGE — Pillow with single seam on its edge, as opposed to squared or box-edged pillow.

KNOCKED DOWN (K.D.) — Furniture sent unassembled from the factory to be put together by store or purchaser.

KNOTTED FRINGE — Fringe with strands of yarn knotted near the heading.

KNOTTED (or KNOTTY) PINE — Once a second-best plank of pine, now sought for the decorative value of its rough knots.

KNOCKED OFF — Furniture industry slang for copying someone else's product.

L

LACQUER — An Oriental technique of varnishing furniture to a brilliant finish, borrowed and popularized by the English and French in the 18th century. Still used today; e.g., lacquered Parsons tables.

LADDER BACK — Chair back with

KNEEHOLE DESK

KLISMOS

KNIFE EDGE PILLOW

LADDER BACK

LAMBREQUIN

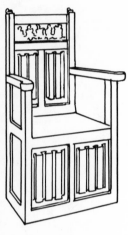

LINEN FOLD DESIGN

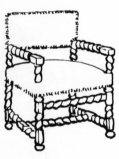

LOUIS XIII CHAIR

LOUIS XV TABLE

a series of ladder-like horizontal supports.

LAMBREQUIN (*lam*-bree-kin) — Decorative frame for a window, originally fabric, now usually made of wood, painted or covered in fabric.

LAMINATE—Two or more materials bonded together under heat and pressure.

LATEX FOAM—Soft, resilient foam rubber much used for upholstered pieces.

LAVABO (la-*va*-bo)—Washbowl, usually porcelain or pottery, hung on wall below matching container that originally held water.

LINEN—Time-honored, durable fabric made from the flax plant.

LINEN FOLD—Stylized motif resembling folded linens carved into furniture, especially during the Tudor period.

LINEN PRESS—Cupboard or chest of drawers for household linens, originally fitted with a board-and-screw press for smoothing the linens.

LIT-CLOS (*lee*-klo)—French for closed bed, i.e., bed with high, wood-paneled back and sides.

LOOP PILE — Carpet with uncut surface yarns. Good in heavy traffic areas.

LOUIS XIII—Or Louis Treize (lu-ee trez). King of France from 1610-1643 while it was still under the spell of the Italian Renaissance. Styles were grand, formal, characterized by rich inlays, carvings, classical motifs.

LOUIS XIV — Or Louis Quatorze (kat-toree). The "Sun King" of France (1643-1715) who built magnificent Versailles palace and filled it with furnishings to match, grandiose, gilded, baroque.

LOUIS XV—Or Louis Quinze (kanz). King of France (1715-1774) whose reign is synonymous

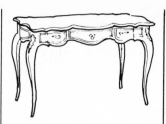

LOUIS XIV CONSOLE

LOUIS XVI BERGERE

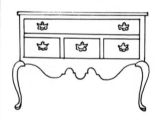

LOW BOY

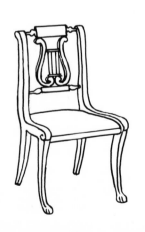

LYRE

with rococo and its delicate, curvilinear, feminine styles.

LOUIS XVI—Or Louis Seize (sez). Ruled France from 1774-1793 and took her back to straight lines and classic motifs.

LOUNGE CHAIR—Any roomy, comfortable chair for relaxing.

LOVE SEAT—Settee or sofa for two.

LOW BOY—Low chest of drawers, often on tall legs.

LOW RELIEF—Design carved on a shallow plane. Also called bas relief.

LOZENGE (*loz*-enge) — Decorative motif shaped like a diamond.

LUCITE (*loo*-cite)—Trade name for clear acrylic plastic.

LUNETTE (loo-*net*)—Band of decoration based on half-moon design.

LYRE (liar) — Musical instrument that became a favorite furniture decoration for Adam, Hepplewhite, Sheraton and especially Duncan Phyfe.

M

MAJOLICA (ma-*jol*-ee-ka)—Tin enameled pottery made in Italy and Spain. Known for its bright colors.

MAN-MADE FIBERS—See Synthetic Fibers.

MANTEL—Projecting shelf across the fireplace top.

MARQUETRY (*mar*-ket-ree)—Elaborate inlay work done with wood, tortoise shell, mother-of-pearl and metals, often depicting scenes.

MARQUISE CHAIR (mar-*keys*) — A wide upholstered armchair of French origin.

MARQUISETTE—Gauze-like sheer fabric popular for glass curtains.

MATELASSE (mat-lah-*say*)—Fabric so woven that it has a quilted surface effect. A favorite for coverlets, drapery, upholstery. From the French, meaning to pad or cushion.

MATE'S CHAIR—Captain's chair minus the added comfort of arms.

MEDALLION—Decorative plaque in embellished wood, metal, stone, etc.

MEDITERRANEAN—The furniture world's name for the popular style originally inspired by Spain and other countries around the Mediterranean Sea, but now flavored with Mexican and South American influences. Massive, pleasantly crude in finish, often featuring wrought iron, and always at home with warm colors, rough textures.

MELAMINE (*mel*-a-meen)—Hard, scratch-resistant plastic found in tableware, laminated table tops, hundreds of other uses. Not a trade name.

MELON-BULB—Bulbous leg turning found on Elizabethan and Jacobean furniture.

MERIDIENNE (mer-ri-den)—Short, French Empire sofa with one arm higher than the other.

MISSION—Named for Spanish missions in early California, this heavy, dark oak furniture was popular at the beginning of this century. Upholstery is leather with hammered copper nailheads.

MITER—To make a corner square without excess bulk.

MODACRYLIC—See Acrylic.

MODERN—An approach to furnishings (art, architecture, etc.) which lets the function of an object dictate its form, eliminating any unnecessary frills and emphasizing the material used. Modern embraces all objects so designed, while "Contemporary" is more of the moment, what's happening now. However, the terms are often used interchangeably, even by the experts.

MEDITERRANEAN CHEST

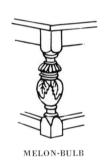

MELON-BULB

MERIDIENNE SOFA

MISSION SOFA

MODULAR—Furniture with various components in standard sizes so they can be easily combined to suit individual needs. Wall units with shelves, bar, desk, etc. components typify the modular approach.

MOHAIR—Great for upholstery because it's so durable, this is a natural fiber from the Angora goat. Often found in blends.

MOIRE (mwa-*ray*)—Fabric given a watermarked appearance by pressing between engraved rollers.

MOLD FRINGE—Trimming made of variously shaped wooden molds sleekly wound with silk, rayon, etc., and suspended from a narrow heading.

MOLDED—Furniture—primarily plastic—actually shaped in a mold, or so smoothly contoured it looks as if it were. Also, many "carved wood" decorations on furnishings are actually molded of plastic, so realistically one can't tell the difference.

MOLLY BOLT—Bolt with wings that flare open when set into wall. Used on plaster walls.

MONK'S CLOTH—Heavy, coarse fabric, tricky to sew because yarns slide but attractive for draperies and upholstery in informal rooms.

MONOCHROMATIC—All of one color, or various shades of one color, as a monochromatic color scheme.

MOQUETTE (mo-*ket*)—Fabric with uncut pile, similar to frisé, woven in small, set patterns of different colors. Made of wool, mohair or heavy cotton for upholstery.

MOROCCO—Fine upholstery leather from goat skin, originally attributed to the Moors.

MORRIS CHAIR—The late 19th century ancestor of today's reclining chairs, this heavy, straight-lined chair has wood frame, adjustable back, loose cushions. William Morris, English artist-architect, is credited with its invention.

MITERED CORNER

MOLD FRINGE

MORRIS CHAIR

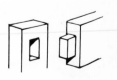

MORTISE AND TENDON

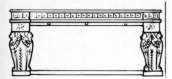

NEO-CLASSIC TABLE

NEO-CLASSIC CHAIR

NESTING TABLES

NIP-TITE HOOK

MORTISE (*mor*-tis) **and TENDON** —Joint used in furniture construction. A cavity is mortised out of one piece of wood and a tendon cut on the other to fit tightly into it.

MOSS FRINGE — Trimming with short, thick, fluffy pile on a narrow heading. Used to edge draperies, or in slipcover seams as welting.

MOTHER-OF-PEARL — The hard internal layer of the oyster and other shells, cut, polished and used for inlays.

MOTIF—Dominant theme of an art work.

MULLION—Wood tracery in glass-paneled doors on bookcases, breakfronts, etc.

MULTI-LEVEL PILE—Carpet with surface yarns at different heights to add texture.

N

NEEDLEPOINT—Embroidery with wool on heavy background fabric. Popular for upholstery, it may be done with fine stitches (petit point) or large stitches (gros point).

NEO-CLASSIC—Literally "new" classic; hence, classic forms revived, as during the French Empire period.

NESTING TABLES—Smallish occasional tables graduated so they slide under each other for storage.

NINON (nee-non)—Sheer voile fabric, usually made of glass fibers when used for curtains.

NIP-TITE PLEATER HOOKS — Used with pleater tape to form and hold pinch pleats in place.

NON-WOVEN FABRICS — These are made by bonding and/or interlocking fibers through chemistry, heat, pressure or some means other than weaving or knitting.

OP ART

ORMOLU

O

OTTOMAN

PAISLEY

N.S.I.D.—National Society of Interior Designers, professional organization of interior designers founded in 1957. Headquarters: 315 E. 62 Street, New York, N.Y. 10021

NUBBY—Yarn with random "nubs" spun in for textured effect.

NYLON—One of the strongest and most versatile of man-made fibers, nylon was first introduced in the U.S. in 1939. Now it's found in curtains, bedspreads, draperies, carpets, stretch fabrics for upholstery, etc. Resistant to moths, mildew, abrasion; dyes beautifully. "Continuous filament" nylon means one long strand; "staple" nylon means many small fibers have been spun together into yarn.

OBJET D'ART (ob-jay-*dar*) — Adopted French term for any small art objects.

OCCASIONAL FURNITURE — Smaller pieces of furniture that come into actual use only occasionally; e.g., pull-up chairs.

OIL FINISH—Furniture finished by rubbing with oil to impart a rich, warm surface which emphasizes the natural wood grains.

OLEFIN (*oh*-lee-fin) (polypropylene and polyethylene) — Fiber manmade from the by-products of the petroleum industry. Light-weight, long-wearing, fade-and-moisture-proof, it has revolutionized carpeting, taking it outdoors and into heavy traffic. Also found in slipcovers and upholstery fabrics.

OMBRE (om-*bray*)—Striped fabric using one color in several shades; used in upholstery.

OP ART—Literally "optic art," a mid-20th-century art movement based on optical illusions produced on canvas through line and color.

ORGANDY—Sheer, crisp fabric often used for glass curtains.

ORIENTAL RUGS — Rich, expensive and long-lived rugs handmade in the Middle and Far East since antiquity. Equally at home in traditional and modern interiors. Generally divided into six major groups: Persian, Bokhara, Turkish, Caucasian, Chinese and Indian. Within each group come rugs named for the particular district or town where they were woven; e.g., Herat, Ispahan, Kashan, Kirman, Kurdistan, Saruk, Hamadan, Shirazes and Senas are among the most notable of Persian carpets.

ORMOLU (*or*-mo-loo)—Gilded bronze, particularly decorative mounts on furniture.

OTTOMAN — An upholstered seat, usually used as a footstool.

OVERLAY — Decorative veneer applied to the surface, as opposed to inlay.

OVOLO (*o*-vo-low)—Band of carved molding with a continuous egg-and-dart motif.

OXBOW FRONT—Furniture fronts curved to resemble an oxbow. 18th-century cabinetmakers in Boston especially favored it.

OYSTERING—Wood veneer cut from cross sections of roots and boughs so they resemble oyster shells.

P

PADDING—The underlay or cushion under carpets. Made of hair, rubber or both combined.

PAISLEY — Multi-colored, comma-shaped motif borrowed not from the East, as you might have supposed, but from the town of Paisley, Scotland, where it first adorned shawls.

PALMETTE (pal-*met*) — Stylized representation of a palm leaf used as ornament.

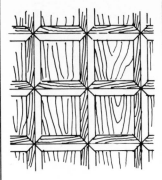

PARQUET

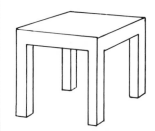

PARSONS TABLE

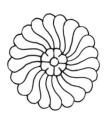

PATERA

PAW FOOT

PANEL — Flat, usually rectangular surface enclosed in a frame. Wall panels of wood or other materials are also enclosed in a framework of molding.

PANNE (pan)—Pile fabric pressed to produce a wonderfully lustrous, shiny surface. Panne is French for "plush."

PAPIER MACHE (paper ma-shay) —Pulp paper molded into decorative items, small pieces of furniture. The French took the idea from the Orient, named it "mashed paper" and popularized it in the 17th century.

PARQUET—Wood flooring laid in geometric patterns.

PARQUETRY—Flooring and, often, furniture surfaces inlaid in patterns.

PARSONS TABLE — Simple, squared-off table developed and named for the Parsons School of Interior Design. Also called T-Square table.

PATERA (*pat*-e-ra)—Round or oval disk ornament, often richly carved.

PATINA (*pat*-e-na) — Soft, mellow finish on furniture and metal caused by age and use.

PAW FOOT—Carved foot resembling an animal's paw, especially a lion's.

PEDESTAL TABLE — Table on a round center support instead of legs.

PEDIMENT—The triangular shape the Greeks devised for their temples adapted to decorative use over doors, atop tall cabinets and highboys, where it may be triangular, rounded or broken at the apex—see Broken Pediment.

PELLON—Trade name for non-woven stiffening material often used for drapery headings.

PEMBROKE TABLE—Small drop-leaf table supposedly named after the English lady who first ordered one in the 1760s.

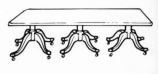

PEDESTAL TABLES

PEDIMENT

PEMBROKE TABLE

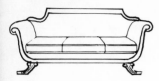

DUNCAN PHYFE SOFA

PIE-CRUST TABLE

PIER GLASS

PILASTER

PENNSYLVANIA DUTCH—A misnomer that has stuck since the first "Deutsch," or German, settlers arrived in Pennsylvania and began making their charmingly primitive painted and now highly prized furniture.

PERMANENT FINISH, PERMANENT PRESS—Terms generally applied to fabric treated to resist shrinking, wrinkles and to maintain creases, pleats, etc.

PERMETTE—Stiff buckram in 11-inch width used for backing cornices.

PETIT POINT—See Needlepoint.

PEWTER—Originally, this alloy of tin and lead served as poor-man's silver. Now it's sought and cherished for its own dull gray good looks.

PHYFE, DUNCAN—One of America's first "name" furniture designers. Although born in Scotland, he worked in New York City from the 1790s until 1847, producing graceful Sheraton-inspired styles. Look for the lyre motif everywhere, brass-tipped dog feet.

PICKLED FINISH—Simulates the whitened look of old pieces of furniture which have had their paint removed, leaving traces of plaster or lime.

PIECE-DYED — Fabric dyed after having been woven.

PIE-CRUST TABLE—Small, tripod-based table with top carved or scalloped a la a pie crust. The 18th-century English fancied them for teatime use.

PIER GLASS—A tall, narrow mirror designed to fit into the pier, the support wall between windows. Occasionally hung over a console table.

PILASTER—Flat-faced column added to a wall or used decoratively on furniture.

PILE — In fabrics and carpets, the tufts of yarn that project from the foundation weave. May be cut, as in a plush carpet and velvet fabric, or left in loops, as in terry-cloth.

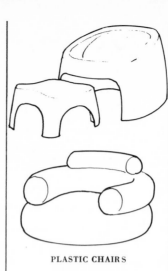

PLASTIC CHAIRS

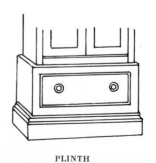

PLATFORM ROCKER

PLINTH

PLASTIC—Discovered back in 1868, plastic is finally being accepted in home furnishings, both as a very successful substitute for natural materials and, most notably, as plastic. Extremely versatile, plastic can be hard and clear (Lucite and Plexiglas) or soft and sit-able (urethane foam cushions and leather-like Naugahyde). Among the plastics you'll most likely find put to home furnishings uses are acrylics, polypropylenes, vinyls, polystyrenes, nylons, polyurethanes, phrenolics and polyesters.

PLATFORM ROCKER—Chair with its rocking apparatus concealed in a platform at its base.

PLEXIGLAS—Registered trademark for see-through acrylic material.

PLINTH — Block base on which a column or chest rests.

PLUSH—Carpet with thick, cut-pile surface. Also, fabric with long pile, often found in upholstery.

PLYWOOD—Layers of wood bonded around a thick central core to form an extraordinarily durable building material. Used for paneling, furniture cores under veneers.

POLYCHROME—Painted in several colors.

POLYESTER—Plastic material that can be molded into tough, rigid shapes, or spun into strong, drip-dry fabrics.

POLYETHYLENE (polly-*eth*-e-lean) — Plastic created from petroleum by-products; can be flexible or rigid, or used in fiber form. Either way, it's strong and durable. See Olefin.

POLYPROPYLENE (polly-*pro*-pa-lean)—Plastic that has two faces—one rigid, the other a durable, fade-proof, moisture-resistant fiber. See Olefin.

POLYSTYRENE — Plastic product often molded into complete pieces of furniture or pressed into decorative components that look like hand-carved wood.

POLYURETHANE—Very adaptable

plastic that can be found molded into either rigid or soft furniture. Like polystyrene, it's often molded into wood-looking decorative elements. Urethane foam is a favorite cushioning material.

POM DECORS — Fluffy pompons strung on cord for use as decorative trimming, "bead" curtains, etc.

PONGEE—Unevenly woven silk (or synthetic) fabric left in its natural tan color. Very durable and, therefore, popular for draw curtains.

POP ART—A somewhat tongue-in-cheek art style that popped out in the 1960s, glorifying everything from comic strips to soup cans. Similar to, but much more fun than the Da-Da movement in the 1930s. Popular as whimsical touch to interiors.

POPLIN—Fabric woven with a fine-rib effect running from selvage to selvage. May be made of natural or man-made fibers, and is popular for draperies.

PORCELAIN—Fine translucent ceramic ware discovered first by the Chinese—hence the term "china." "Bone china" has bone ash added to the clay mixture.

POROMERICS—Vinyl fabrics constructed to "breathe."

PORTER'S CHAIR (or watchman's chair)—Large upholstered chair with a high, curved hood to keep off drafts. An 18th-century invention.

POTPOURRI — In decorating, a pleasant medley of styles. See Eclectic.

POUDREUSE (poo-*dreuze*) — Powder or toilet table, as the French would have it.

PRE-PASTED—Wallpaper pre-glued so you need only moisten and hang.

PRESSED GLASS — Glass decorated by pressing into ornamental molds.

PRIE DIEU (pree-dee-*you*)—"Pray God" is its name and that's just why this high-backed low chair has a

POM DECORS

POP ART

PORTER'S CHAIR

FRENCH PROVINCIAL

padded rail for the elbows. Dates from 16th-century Italy.

PRIMARY COLORS — The three colors — red, blue and yellow — from which all others are derived.

PRIMITIVE — Simple, unsophisticated design and execution. Much Early American furniture is primitive. So are the paintings of Grandma Moses, even though she lived in the 20th century.

PROVINCIAL—Copies made in the provinces, or country, of furnishings popular in the more sophisticated cities; hence, rustic but usually charming.

PSYCHE—Name for both a cheval mirror found in France during the Empire Period, and for an upholstered sofa dating from about 1840.

PSYCHEDELIC ART—Fluid, Day-Glo art, unreal as a dream, arising in the late 1960s, supposedly from images seen through hallucinatory drugs. This art is free and fun when added sparingly to a room.

PULL-UP CHAIR—Occasional arm chair to be pulled into use as needed.

Q

QUARRIES — Square or diamond-shaped glass panes traditionally used in English bookcase doors.

QUATREFOIL — Stylized four-leaf clover design.

QUEEN ANNE—Queen of England for just 12 years (1702-14), she's immortalized in design history by the graceful, delicate furniture she favored. Look for cabriole legs, carved fans and shells.

QUILTED — Pattern stitched so it joins two layers of fabric with padding sandwiched in between. Quilted fabric adds luxury to bedspreads, upholstery, even walls.

PRIMITIVE TABLE

PSYCHEDELIC ART

QUATREFOIL

QUEEN ANNE CHAIR

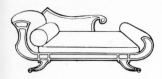

RECAMIER

REEDING

ENGLISH REGENCY CHAIR

RENAISSANCE CASSONE

R

RANCH WINDOW—Long window placed high in the wall of contemporary homes.

RAT-TAIL FRINGE — Decorative edging with swagged loops woven to a heading.

RATTAN—An Oriental palm woven into airy, decorative wicker-work furniture.

RAYON — Grandmother of all the man-made fibers (1916) and looking younger than ever in hundreds of household uses, from trimmings to carpets.

READING STAND — Small table with top that adjusts to hold a book.

RECAMIER — Chaise longue with one end higher than the other. Named after Madame Recamier who reclines upon such a chaise in her famous portrait by Jacques Louis David, art director of France under Napoleon.

RECLINER—Lounge chair, usually with a built-on footrest, which adjusts to many positions.

REEDING — Elongated ornamentation similar to fluting but with the parallel lines in relief.

REGENCY, ENGLISH — Glittering reign of George, Prince of Wales, as Regent from 1811 to 1820. Even earlier, furnishings began to reflect the growing interest in ancient cultures that characterizes the Regency style—Greek, Roman and Egyptian motifs predominate, with animal forms and Chinese designs close behind.

REGENCY, FRENCH—Period from the death of Louis XIV in 1715 to 1723 when Louis XV took over as king. Furniture of the period reflects the relaxation of the Sun King's pomp into the lighter, elegant pieces of the Louis XV style.

RELATED COLORS — Colors that fall next to each other on the color wheel and are, therefore, related in

RIBBAND

ROCKING CHAIR

ROCOCO ORNAMENT

ROLL-TOP DESK

hue. A related color scheme is built around such kindred colors.

RELIEF—Ornament above the surface it decorates. High (haut) relief is decidedly above the surface, low (bas) only slightly.

RENAISSANCE—The rebirth, literally, of intellectual and artistic endeavor in Europe from the 14th to the 17th centuries. Renaissance furniture is characteristically massive, ornate, heavily carved.

REP (or repp)—Fabric with a ribbed effect. Often used for draperies, upholstery.

REPEAT — On printed fabric, the size of one complete pattern motif.

REPOUSSE (ray-poo-*say*) — Embossed relief work on metal. The design is hammered out from within.

REPRODUCTION — Modern copy of yesteryear's style.

RESTORATION—Period following the restoration of Charles II to the English throne in 1660 when furnishings were characterized by elaborately carved crowns, supposedly to mark the event.

RIBBAND—Chair back composed of interlaced ribbons. A Chippendale favorite.

ROCKING CHAIR—America popularized this homey, comfortable chair on runners.

ROCOCO (row-*ko*-ko) — Exuberant, asymmetrical, ornate design. The original Rococo period developed in 18th-century France where it was based on such natural forms as rocks and shells (rocaille and coquille)—whence comes the name.

ROLL-TOP DESK—Desk with tambour lid that rolls down over the working area.

ROMAN SHADE — Window treatment similar to Austrian shade but with straight tailored folds instead of swags.

ROMAYNE WORK (row-main) — Carved medallion heads or knobs used for furniture ornament, especially during the Jacobean and Restoration periods.

ROOM DIVIDER — A piece of furniture, screen, anything, in fact, that serves to partition a room physically or psychologically.

ROSETTE — Ornament of stylized leaves radiating from a center point. May be round, elliptical or square.

ROUNDABOUT CHAIR — A corner chair with the legs at the front, back and one on each side of the seat, which is placed on the diagonal.

RUSH SEAT — Seat woven from rushes, a marsh grass. Usually found on primitive, country furniture.

RYA RUG (ree-a) — Shag rugs handwoven in Scandinavia, often with modernized peasant designs. Named for the method of construction, the Rya or Flossa weave.

SAARINEN TABLE — Sculptured plastic pedestal table with matching chairs designed by architect Eero Saarinen in 1960; all are now classics of the modern style.

SAILCLOTH — Very durable canvaslike fabric used occasionally for furniture covers.

SANFORIZED — Trademark for a process that reduces shrinkage in fabrics to less than 1 per cent.

SARAN — Very heavy, weather-resistant, man-made fiber used for outdoor upholstery.

SASH CURTAIN — See Glass Curtain.

SATEEN — Cotton fabric with a glossy surface and dull back often used for slipcovers, drapery linings.

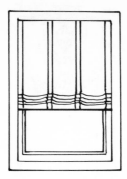

ROMAN SHADE

ROSETTE

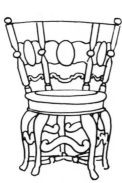

ROUNDABOUT CHAIR

SAARINEN TABLE

SATIN — Lustrous-surfaced fabric with dull reverse side originally made of silk in Zaytun, China. The name remains but most satin today is woven from synthetics, sometimes backed with cotton for durability. "Antique satin" is usually dull, heavy and richly textured. A popular fabric for home decorating.

SAVONAROLA (sav-a-na-roll-a) — Italian Renaissance X-shaped chair.

SAVONNERIE RUGS (sa-von-nre) — The aristocrats of rugs made in the West; handmade, pile-surfaced, following the rich designs established when Henry IV of France set up rug production in a former soap factory (savonnerie) at Paris in the early 1600s.

SCALLOPED BESTPLEAT — Pleater tape for cafe curtains, alternating scallops and pinch pleats. See Bestpleat.

SCANDINAVIAN MODERN — Simple but elegant furniture with a hand-sculpted look. Generally devoid of ornamentation so attention focuses on the beautiful, oiled woods, usually teak, walnut or rosewood.

SCONCE — Ornamental wall bracket to hold light bulbs or candles.

SCRIM — Light, open, cheese-cloth-like fabric used for curtains.

SCROLLWORK — Ornamentation based on a curving or spiraling line. A scroll foot on furniture curves in such a line. A scroll pediment is a broken pediment with each half ending in a scroll, usually with a finial between.

SECONDARY COLORS — Green, violet and orange; each color is made by mixing two primary colors.

SECRETARY (or secretaire) — Desk with a drop front for writing, drawers below and bookcase above.

SECTIONAL — Furniture (usually upholstered) designed so that it can be used separately or grouped into various arrangements.

SAVONAROLA CHAIR

SCONCE

SCROLLWORK

SECRETARY

SEMAINIER

SERPENTINE

SETTLE

SHERATON CHAIR

SELF-COVERED SEAT DECK — Area under the cushions on upholstered furniture covered to match the rest of the piece, usually on quality furniture.

SELVAGE—Woven edge of fabric or carpet.

SEMAINIER (sa-man-*yeh*) — Tall, narrow chest with seven drawers, one for each day in the week, as the French word for week, "semain," implies.

SERPENTINE—Undulating. A buffet desk, etc., with a curvy front.

SETTEE—Long seat with side arms and back, sometimes upholstered, that evolved into today's sofa.

SETTLE—Ancestor of the sofa, an all-wood bench with high back and solid arms. Often the seat was a box with a hinged lid.

SHAG—Carpet with long, loose pile.

SHAKER FURNITURE — Simply designed, admirably made furnishings by the Shakers, a religious sect in Eastern America during the 18th and 19th centuries. Very much to contemporary taste, copies of Shaker furniture are produced by manufacturers today.

SHEARED (or tip-sheared)—Carpet pile cut to produce a plush surface.

SHELL MOTIF — Ornament in the shape of cockle shell.

SHERATON, THOMAS—The last of the great furniture designers who made England famous during the Georgian Period, Sheraton (1751-1806) has been called the "high priest of the straight line." His designs are simple, squared off instead of curvilinear; his motifs inspired by the classics. Look for square chair backs, slender tapering legs. An inventive man, Sheraton designed multipurpose furniture—desks that turned into tables, stools into small library stairs, etc. He also published a book of furniture designs that spread both his fame and his style (America's Duncan Phyfe was a great admirer), but never won him financial success.

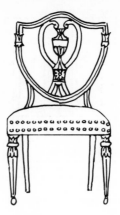

SHIELD BACK

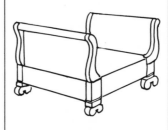

SLEIGH BED

SLIPPER CHAIR

SHIELD BACK—Chair back shaped like an open heraldic shield with carved ribbons, feathers, etc. Hepplewhite loved it.

SHIRRING — Fabric gathered in small folds on thread or a rod, or with special tape.

SHIR-RITE—Flat tape with woven-in cords to simplify shirring. Available in one-inch and four-inch (4-Cord Shir Tape) widths.

SHOJI SCREEN (show-je)—Plastic covered, translucent screen borrowed from the Orient, where it was covered with rice paper.

SIDE CHAIR—Small armless dining chair.

SIDEBOARD—Originally a board, literally, for the storage and serving of food; now usually has doors or drawers beneath for storage and open display shelves above. Hepplewhite is credited with the transformation.

SISAL (*sigh*-sal) — Straw-like fiber from a tropical plant often used for padding, summer rugs.

SKIRT—See Apron.

SLEIGH BED—American, 19th century bed with ends rolled up scroll-like, reminiscent of sleigh fronts.

SLIPCOVER—Removable cover for upholstered furniture.

SLIPPER CHAIR — Low, armless upholstered chair supposedly designed for putting on one's shoes.

SLUBS—Thick, uneven yarns woven into fabric for surface interest.

SOFA—Long, upholstered seat for at least three persons.

SOFA-BED—Sofa which converts into a bed.

SOFA TABLE—Long narrow table with drawers, drop-leaf ends. Popular in England, beginning in the 18th century.

SPADE FOOT — Square, tapering foot.

SPANISH — Massive, richly ornamented furniture that has changed little throughout Spanish history. Look for tooled leather, wrought-iron stretchers, ornamental nailheads. See Mediterranean.

SPANISH FOOT—Foot shaped like an inward-curving scroll or a hand resting on its knuckles. William and Mary favored it, and 18th-century America adopted it.

SPATTER-DASH—Random splashing done in several colors or shades, mainly in flooring.

SPINDLE—Long thin, often carved rod found on chair backs.

SPLAT—The major vertical support in a chair back.

SPLINT SEAT — Seat woven from thin strips of wood.

SPLIT-LEVEL — Contemporary house design with rooms at several levels.

SPOOL TURNING — Continuous turning shaped like rows of spools. Found on chair legs, bed posts.

SPOON BACK—Queen Anne chair back curved like a spoon to fit the body's contour.

SPRING EDGE—Upholstered furniture with springs supporting the edge instead of padded wood.

SPRINGS — Coiled wire or flat S-shaped metal strips used to give comfort, resiliency to upholstered furniture, mattresses.

STACKING FURNITURE—Pieces designed so they can actually be stacked on top of each other when not in use—chairs, tables, etc. Or units that are stacked, building-block style, to form a free-standing wall system.

STAINLESS STEEL—Steel alloyed with chromium. Used handsomely on modern furniture.

STENCIL—Method of decorating by painting through a cut-out pattern.

SPANISH FOOT

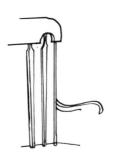

SPINDLE

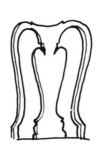

SPLAT

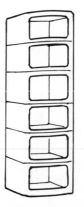

STACKING FURNITURE

STEP TABLE—Occasional table in two step-like tiers.

STERLING—Silverware that is 92½ per cent pure silver.

STOCK-DYED—Fabric woven from fibers dyed before spinning into yarn.

STRAPWORK — Highly formalized carving on a band of ornament, somewhat suggestive of interlaced bands or straps.

STRETCH FABRICS—Used for upholstery that fits like skin to curving contemporary furniture. Usually made of long-wearing nylon.

STRETCHER—Wood or metal strip connecting furniture legs.

STRIE (stri-ay) — Fabric with random stripes just slightly different in color from the background.

STRIPPABLE—Wallpaper designed to be easily removed.

STUCCO—Plaster or cement coating for walls.

STUDS—Large, decorative nailheads.

STUMP — Front support of a chair arm.

STYLIZING—Reduced to a pleasing design rather than representing nature, e.g., stylized flowers on wallpaper.

SUITE—Set of matched furniture for individual rooms. Before today's eclecticism, almost all furniture was bought in suites.

SWAG — Draped fabric used at a window, often with side jabots. Anything — flowers, garlands, ribbons — hung in a festoon.

SWAG BALL FRINGE—Large ball fringe with alternating balls and swags.

SWATCH—Sample cutting of fabric, paint color, etc.

SWING-LEG TABLE — Table with hinged or folding legs that swing out to support drop leaves.

STRAPWORK

STRETCHER

STUMP

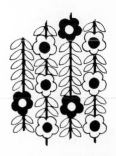

STYLIZED DESIGN

299

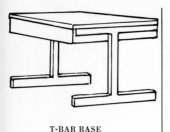

T-BAR BASE

TEA CADDY

TIER TABLE

TIFFANY LAMP

SYMMETRICAL—Design with both halves exactly alike or perfectly balanced in mass and detail.

SYNTHETIC FIBERS—Fibers manmade chemically from raw materials found in nature and used to make fabrics with qualities not always possible in natural fibers. See individual fiber listings.

T

TABLET CHAIR — Chair with one wide, flat wooden arm for writing.

TABORET (or tabouret) (*tab*-oh-ret)—Low stool or stand.

TAFFETA—Fine, plain-weave fabric named for the Persian fabric taftan. Originally silk, now made of synthetic fibers. Good for draperies.

TAMBOUR — Flexible door of thin wooden strips mounted on heavy fabric. Slides open and closed in a groove, as in a roll-top desk.

TAPESTRY — A figured, multi-colored fabric popular and long-lived as upholstery.

TASSEL FRINGE—Trimming with tassels looped to a woven heading.

T-BAR BASE—Base for table, chair, chest, etc., shaped like an upside-down T with vertical support attached to a horizontal piece on the floor.

TEA CADDY—Small box for storing tea, usually equipped with lock and key since, in the 17th century, tea was an expensive luxury. Caddy is a corruption of the word "kati," the Malay measure of about a pound of tea.

TEA CART—Mobile server that has rolled from the 18th century parlor, where it was a teatime fixture, onto the modern scene as a bar or barbeque accessory.

TEAR DROP—See Drop Handle.

TERRAZZO (ter-*raht*-so)—Concrete

TILT-TOP TABLE

TORCHERE

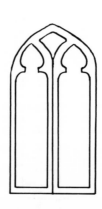

TRACERY

surfacing for floors and walls made of, or resembling, crushed marble and cement.

TESTER—Canopy over a four-poster bed.

THONET—See Bentwood.

TICKING—Closely woven fabric with stripes on a white ground. Time-honored mattress-and-pillow cover, it has emerged as a popular, durable drapery and upholstery fabric.

TIER TABLE — Table with tiers graduated in size to smallest at the top. Usually has a pedestal or tripod base.

TIFFANY GLASS — Hand-blown glass made by Louis Comfort Tiffany in New York during the late 1890's, characterized by its swirling Art Nouveau forms, wavy, iridescent colors. Back in vogue with a smash, especially in lamps, in the 1960's.

TILT-TOP TABLE—Pedestal table with top hinged so it can be tilted into a vertical position to save space when it's not in use.

TINTS — Colors close to white in value.

TOILE DE JOUY (twal-de-*jwee*) — Popular toile fabrics of linen, cotton or silk printed with pastoral or historical scenes, usually in only one color. First produced in the late 1700's in Jouy, France, near Versailles, and still in great demand.

TONGUE-AND-GROOVE—Joint in furniture construction in which a projecting tongue on one piece fits into a groove on the other.

TORCHERE (tor-*shair*)—Floor lamp which throws all its light upward. Descendent of the pedestal or candlestand of yester-year.

TORTOISE SHELL — Shell of the sea turtle, popular for inlays; also anything printed to resemble tortoise shell.

TRACERY—Delicate openwork patterns of circular shapes and intersecting arcs, first borrowed from Gothic stonework.

TRADITIONAL—Style of decorating inspired by the past.

TRANSITIONAL—Style of decorating showing the transition from one style to another and containing elements of both.

TRAPUNTO (tra-*pun*-to) — Upholstery fabric quilted in high relief over a layer of filler inserted between the surface fabric and a muslin backing.

TRAVERSE ROD—Curtain rod designed to pull draperies open and closed across the window.

TRAY TABLE — Serving tray supported by a folding stand. Also called a butler's tray, it originated in the 18th century, returned in the 20th as the TV table.

TREFOIL (*tree*-foil)—Three-leaf ornament borrowed from Gothic times.

TRESTLE TABLE — Long, heavy table supported by uprights at each end attached to a heavy horizontal stretcher.

TRIACETATE—See Acetate.

TRIPLE DRESSER—Long dresser with triple tiers of drawers or compartments.

TRIPOD TABLE — Small table mounted on a pedestal with three outward turning legs.

TRIPTYCH (*trip*-tick) — Hinged mirror, picture, screen, etc., with three panels.

TRIVET—Small three-legged metal stand designed to hold dishes.

TROMPE L'OEIL (tromp-*lay*) — French for "fool the eye"; painted decorations that look so real they do, indeed, fool the eye.

TRUNDLE BED—Low rolling bed that stores under a larger bed.

TUB CHAIR—Large round lounge chair.

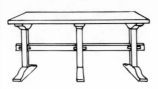

TRESTLE TABLE

TRAVERSE ROD

TRIPOD TABLE

TUB CHAIR

TUDOR PERIOD — Historically speaking, the Tudor Period in England lasted from 1500-1558, but the tastes of the time carry on for another hundred years through the Elizabethan and Jacobean Periods. Furniture is mainly oak, massive and squarish, but ornately carved. Look for bulbous legs, low stretchers, the Tudor Rose, that stylized carving of a rose which symbolized the Tudor kings.

TUFTING—Both a method of upholstering and a kind of carpet construction. In the former, the layers of material are sewn together, often caught to a button. Such tufting often creates a design on the furniture—"biscuit tufting" is rows of squares, for example. Tufted carpets are made by drawing yarn through the backing material with machine-driven needles, leaving surface loops which may then be cut or uncut. A relatively new and widely used method of construction, it produces durable floor coverings.

TURNING — Ornamentation produced by turning wood—e.g., chair legs—on a lathe and shaping it as it spins.

TUXEDO SOFA — Sofa with rectangular side arms or panels the same height as the back.

TWEED—Rough textured fabric of wool, cotton or synthetic yarns, either multicolored or monotone. Named for the Tweed River separating England from Scotland, where tweed was originally homespun. Used for upholstery.

TWIST — Cut pile which is corkscrewed to give a pebbly effect to a carpet surface.

U

UNDER CONSTRUCTION — Springs in the back and seat of upholstered furniture.

UREA (u-*ree*-a) — Sturdy, scratch-resistant plastic closely akin to melamine.

TUDOR ARMOIRE

TUFTING

TURNING

TUXEDO SOFA

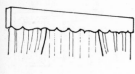

VALANCE

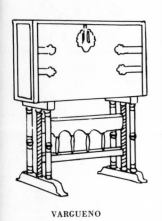

VARGUENO

VICTORIAN CHAIR

URETHANE FOAM—See Polyurethane.

V

VALANCE — Decorative horizontal strip across window top. Conceals drapery headings, hardware, sometimes light sources. Also the drapery on a canopy bed.

VALUE—The lightness or darkness of a color.

VAN DER ROHE, MIES (row, mees) — Twentieth-century architect who designed clean-lined modern furniture. See Barcelona Chair.

VANITY (or vanity table)—A dressing table.

VARGUENO (var-*gay*-neo)—Spanish desk-cabinet on a stand; has a drop-front.

VAT DYE—Chemically activated dye which imparts virtually fade-proof colors to fabrics.

VELCRO—A clever fastening device on the order of snap-tape but utilizing two nylon strips which adhere to each other when pressed together.

VELOUR (ve-*loor*)—Fabric similar to velvet but with deeper pile.

VELVET — Fabric with thick, short surface pile, plain back. Once made of all silk, now contains a mixture of fibers. Heavy velvet is often used for upholstery.

VELVET CARPET—Carpet named for the type of loom upon which it is woven.

VELVETEEN—Cotton velvet.

VENEER — A method of furniture construction where handsomely grained woods or other decorative materials are applied in thin sheets over a sturdy, but less showy, foundation material.

VICTORIAN SOFA

VITRINE

WAINSCOT CHAIR

VENETIAN BLINDS — Window shades made of thin slats of wood or metal strung on tapes so they open and close.

VENETIAN FURNITURE — Extravagantly ornamental furniture produced in Italy during the late Renaissance. Often gilded and painted.

VERTICAL BLINDS — A kind of slender venetian blind turned on its side.

VICTORIAN—The period from 1837 to 1901 when Queen Victoria ruled England and generally bad taste ruled interior design. The era is marked by extravagant eclecticism, more accurately called hodge-podge. Furnishings were as stiff and formal as the manners of the age, but not always without a kind of charm that makes them enjoyable in small doses today. Look for marble tops, tufted upholstery, blown-up curves and swells.

VINYL—One of the most versatile of plastics, vinyl can be flexible, rigid or blown into foam. Expanded and supported vinyl, backed with cloth and urethane foam, makes durable, leather-like upholstery. Vinyl coatings give washability to wall coverings. Vinyl floor tiles are the most durable floor coverings available (vinyl asbestos tiles offer good looks and wear at a more modest price). Inflatable vinyls, clear and in colors, account for some of the most fun furniture on the modern scene.

VIS-A-VIS (*veez*-a-vee)—Two seats, attached in the center, but facing opposite directions.

VITRINE (vee-*treen*)—Curio display cabinet with glass doors and, occasionally, glass sides and top for all-round viewing.

VOILE (voil) — Light, transparent fabric used for glass curtains.

W

WAINSCOT (*wain*-skot) — Wooden paneling for interior walls; especially paneling that reaches only part-way to the ceiling. The word derives from the term for "wagon-boarding," describing the flat type of panels used.

WAINSCOT CHAIR — Chair with flat seat and heavy back paneled like wainscot.

WALL PLUG — Special screw for plaster walls.

WALL SYSTEM—Inventive way to put walls to work, consisting of interchangeable wall-hung or free-standing units—cabinets, desks, shelves, etc.

WARDROBE—Large cupboard with doors and shelves used for hanging clothes in pre-closet rooms.

WASH STAND—Forerunner of the bathroom sink, a cupboard or table with basin in the top covered by a lid.

WEBBING — Interwoven bands of burlap (or rubber or plastic) used to support the springs in upholstering.

WEDGWOOD—Josiah W. Wedgwood (1735-95), perhaps the most famous name in English pottery; best known for his cameos against a "Wedgwood blue" background.

WEGNER, HANS—One of the first and foremost Danish designers whose beautifully carved chair (1949) fired American enthusiasm for Scandinavian modern furniture.

WELT—Fabric-covered cord sewn into slipcover seams, etc. for a finished appearance.

WHAT-NOT — Stand with open shelves for showing off bric-a-brac.

WHEAT EAR — Carved ornament representing ears of wheat; a Hepplewhite favorite.

WHORL (hwirl)—A circular decorative ornament with "whirling" carvings inside. Also, a spiral turning.

WICKER—Furniture woven of willow or other pliant fibers, once *de riqueur* for the front porch but now at home throughout the house.

WASH STAND

WEDGWOOD CAMEO

WEGNER CHAIR

WHEAT EAR

WILTON—A type of loom used for carpet construction; hence a carpet with cut wool pile and a cotton back made on such a loom.

WILLIAM AND MARY—Period (1689-1702) when English furnishings began to grow lighter and less ornate, as French influence replaced the Dutch baroque of the Restoration period preceding it. Look for furniture legs shaped like trumpets, flat serpentine stretchers, double-hooded cabinets and delicate "seaweed" marquetry. Walnut was used almost exclusively.

WINDOW SEAT—Now a built-in seat under a window, derived from an upholstered two-seater with arms but no back originally used in a window nook.

WINDOW SHADES — The Cinderella of decorating, the window shade has gone from a dull utilitarian window covering to a high interior fashion with exciting new laminates, shapes and trims.

WINDSOR CHAIR—Windsor, England, gave birth to this jaunty, all-wood chair, but it won its fame in America, where the colonists turned out many varieties; comb-back (named for the shape of the top rail), hoop-or bow-back, which have bentwood rails. The seat is saddle-shaped of solid wood or made of rush, and legs and spindles are set in at a rakish angle. There is also a Windsor rocker.

WING CHAIR — An upholstered chair with high back and projecting sides designed to keep off the drafts in 18th-century houses but still popular in today's centrally heated homes.

WINTHROP DESK — A Chippendale slant-top desk supposedly named for Governor Winthrop of Massachusetts in the 17th century.

X

X-STRETCHER—Crossed stretchers on furniture, either straight or curved.

WINDOW SEAT

WINDSOR CHAIR

WING CHAIR

X-STRETCHER